T
Seven Deadly Sins of Management

CW01590225

The Seven Deadly Sins of Management

Malcolm Peel and Bob Norton

Illustrations by Peter Allen

ARROW
BUSINESS BOOKS

Published by Arrow Books in 1994

1 3 5 7 9 10 8 6 4 2

© Malcolm Peel and Bob Norton 1994

Malcolm Peel and Bob Norton have asserted their rights under the Copyright, Designs and Patents Act, 1988 to be identified as the authors of this work

All characters in this publication are fictitious and any resemblance to real persons, living or dead, is purely coincidental

This book is sold subject to the condition that it shall not, by way of trade or otherwise, be lent, resold, hired out or otherwise circulated without the publisher's prior consent in any form of binding or cover other than that in which it is published and without a similar condition including this condition being imposed on the subsequent purchaser

Published by Arrow Books Limited
20 Vauxhall Bridge Road, London SW1V 2SA

Random House Australia (Pty) Limited
20 Alfred Street, Milsons Point, Sydney,
New South Wales 2061, Australia

Random House New Zealand Limited
18 Poland Road, Glenfield,
Auckland 10, New Zealand

Random House South Africa (Pty) Limited
PO Box 337, Bergvlei, South Africa

Random House UK Limited Reg. No. 954009

ISBN 0 09 943911 5

Typeset in Bembo by SX Composing Limited, Rayleigh, Essex
Printed and bound in Great Britain by Cox & Wyman Ltd,
Reading, Berks

Contents

In the Beginning

Thirty years after his baptism of fire into management, (see: *The Ten Commandments of Management*) Andrew Buckden is at the peak of his career. The lessons he learnt in the first six months at United Group had burned into his soul and provided him with the foundation for all his achievements.

During those thirty years Andrew had turned United Group from a slumbering giant into an international leader in garden gnomes. His capacity for creating new markets and huge profits had earned him an envied reputation. His name was rarely missing from the pages of the business press.

Relubbus, as we know, was condemned for his failure to retraining. Thirty years represents but a nano-second in the struggle for management destruction, but the word was that Relubbus was now refreshed and eager for work. Unlike Andrew, Relubbus had suffered; such was his fate. He was now revitalized for the intrigue and deceit of destruction.

Barripper had not been in touch with Relubbus, his nephew. Buckden's success had wounded Barripper who had had to content himself with the downfall of governments and the bankruptcy of nations – a far easier task than the destruction of managers. But Barripper had not forgotten the name of Andrew Buckden and his anger was terrible as the Watchers reported his growing achievements.

Recently the reports of the Watchers had brought glimmers of hope to Barripper. Buckden had revealed the first signs of vulnerability, a change in his resolve, a new ambition. Barripper recognized the symptoms and rubbed his

Allen

hands in anticipation. The Management Destruction Unit had a programme of awesome power at its disposal. Buckden was ripe for attack. Barripper was ready to guide Relubbus in tempting Andrew to commit each of the Seven Deadly Sins in turn.

The Players

Andrew Buckden: Chief Executive of United Group, world leading supplier of garden gnomes. Buckden survived the onslaught of Barripper and Relubbus thirty years ago. Buckden's industry has recognized his success in turning United Group into a market leader, but Buckden now desires higher recognition as the crowning glory to a successful career.

Barripper: Archtempter whose role is to destroy managers. As head of the Management Destruction Unit (MDU), his most significant personal contributions caused havoc in the Hundred Years War, the decay process established in the Industrial Revolution, and the training and development of Attila the Hun. It was Barripper who invented the concept of the planet as global dustbin. Would rate the destruction of Buckden as a notable achievement.

Relubbus: Junior Tempter who does all the dirty work. Failed miserably to trap Buckden at the beginning of his career. Gained centuries of experience in thirty years' retraining.

His greatest asset is the ability to appear anywhere, anytime, in the guise of a manager. His greatest drawback is a tendency to blow his cover in outbursts of exuberance. Needs to snare Buckden this time round to maintain his street-cred.

Chapter 1

Trendiness

'A good catchword can obscure analysis for fifty years.'
WENDELL WILLKIE

My dear Relubbus

The pleasurable anticipation of evil to come that these three words give to your aged uncle is greater than you will understand. You know the disappointment I experienced when you failed, despite my guidance, in your first assignment as a Junior Tempter. You will remember the efforts I made, abusing my authority as a senior and respected member of the Lowerarchy, to have your punishment for this failure mitigated. You will have guessed the depth of my sorrow when this failed to weigh against the need for your comprehensive reprogramming at the hands of the Infernal Retraining and Redeployment Executive (IRRE).

I have followed every stage of your progress through the purifying fires and interactive seminars of IRRE. Indeed, I had full reports from the Course Tutors of all that was happening to you delivered to me annually. It would be too much to say that I suffered with you. In fact, I must admit to twinges of delight at the descriptions of the more ingenious forms of correction to which you were subject. I had not realized the progress that the IRRE had made in recent years, and the subtlety of some of the latest techniques for Tempter retraining.

But to turn to your future. You will have been told that

your first assignment now you have requalified will be the destruction of the manager who caused your previous downfall, Andrew Buckden. This is standard procedure, and the reasons for it are sound; it would be embarrassing in the extreme if any manager, on reaching the great Boardroom in the sky, could plead that he had outwitted one of our people. It is now up to you to ensure that this does not occur, and that you use this second chance to drag him to destruction. Should you fail, the consequences will make your thirty years of attendance on IRRE seminars seem like a Harvard professor's summer vacation. The fact that you are my nephew would then do nothing to lessen your punishment; rather, it would make it even more dire; from those to whom much has been given, much is required.

Since he escaped your clutches all those years ago, Andrew Buckden has prospered. From a raw graduate trainee, he has risen to the height of Chairman and Chief Executive of the United Group. His salary is at the level of twenty of his productive workers. His office would accommodate a section of ten of his designers. His company car is the size of the buses provided to pick up his

workers from the nearby council estate. His package is the envy of his fellow members of the Institute of Directors. He is entitled to as many free garden gnomes per year as he, his family and friends can use.

As he has prospered, so has the United Group. It has, largely as a result of his skilled leadership, become the leading supplier of garden gnomes and figurines worldwide. Through an aggressive strategy of asset-stripping, reverse cash bids, hostile takeovers, insider dealing, industrial espionage, and creative use of the employee pension fund, its position has become second to none.

The mission statement of the United Group is:

> Every householder in the world shall have at least one United gnome in his possession, even though he lacks a garden to put it in.

When it was first enunciated by Buckden, it was a matter for derision. Thanks to the marketing strategies he has put in place, this is now within measurable distance of becoming true. Anticipating the inevitable weakening of demand within the developed world, the United Group targeted the people of the developing nations. Its brilliant team created a brand image of world-wide potency. Percy, the fishing gnome, is now recognized instantly by people of all ages, socio-economic categories and ethnic origins worldwide. Percy has been inextricably grafted on to the universal pop culture of the young, and from there transplanted into the lives of their elders. Primitive villagers in the high Andes, the poorer parts of Sri Lanka and Uzbekistan share the same warm family feelings for Percy. None of their houses and gardens (if they have them), their sheds, shacks, tents or tin-roofed lean-tos feel complete without Percy. Those who do not have him feel their life is incomplete. Thefts galore, blackmail and murders have been committed for Percy. In some areas, wealth is not now judged by money, nor the number of animals, but by the number of United garden gnomes owned by the head of family. The very name of the group has been used to create an image of universal togetherness.

The group's manufacturing policies have been based on a number of proven principles. It has created a series of fashions for its products, to reduce their lifespan. It has used the techniques of value engineering to develop products that meet customer needs at minimum cost; they have been designed to disintegrate just before the point at which the average customer has started to tire of them. It has bought raw materials at rock bottom prices from defenceless producers in subsistence economies. It has continuously moved its production facilities round the world in search of the most easily exploitable sources of labour. Having squeezed massive subsidies out of national governments and international agencies on the pretext of generating employment and prosperity, it has pulled out, closed up and moved on.

These and the other techniques of modern global management, have put United in an apparently impregnable position. You may see this double success an obstacle to your task, but the reverse is true. Your abysmal failures when first responsible for his destruction gave Buckden an opportunity which he grasped. I understand that Buckden paid two hack writers to glorify his story in a totally untruthful account of that sad episode. Your chance has now come. He is more vulnerable than he appears. Buckden has moved into the ranks of Top Management.

He is, however, not recognized outside his industry. He has no title, no 'honour' (as these trivial little people call meaningless additions to their address), he is on no Royal Commissions. He is not, in a phrase we invented some years ago, one of the 'Great and Good'. He and his second wife Jane are desperate for him to 'get his K' (ie to be allowed to call himself 'Sir Andrew'). This step, between being the successful manager you allowed him to become and a Top Person, has now become an obsession. This is the chink in his armour; it is by this Achilles' heel that we shall snare him and haul him into the warm place we have reserved for him.

Buckden outwitted you by obeying the Ten Commandments of Management as those hacks described the falsification of your first and only failure. You must now ensure he is condemned to perdition through tempting him to commit one or more of the Seven Deadly Sins of Management. Against one in his position, these are weapons of enormous, almost irresistible, power.

Of course managers are not, as a class, immediately associated with sin. This is mainly because sin is thought of as enjoyable, something that no one in their right mind would think of management. But it is also because managers are a class of human (I use the word loosely) which has hidden its sinfulness by legalizing it. (The other class that has done this with outstanding success is, of course, the legal profession.) But of all areas of human activity, management is without doubt the most sinful. Management hardly existed until we had stimulated what humans call the 'Industrial Revolution' some two hundred years ago. Before this, the air was clean, the waters unpolluted, the earth's resources unexploited. It is managers who have changed this; the excesses of the modern world are the excesses of management. The air humans now breathe and the water they drink are defiled, the irreplaceable resources of their tiny patch of the time-bound universe plundered.

The most amusing aspect of the situation is that humans see these changes as beneficial. The countries that have led the process of managerial destruction – the 'developed' world as we have taught them to call it – revel in their orgy, and the rest – the 'developing countries' – yearn to follow. Managers preen themselves on their success, and the masses worship them.

Few realize that it is our labours, spearheaded by the All Lowest Himself, that inspired this process. Indeed, not only managers but the majority of the human race no longer even believe we exist. This, of course, is exactly as we would wish. As long as humans believe that their problems spring from causes which they can, eventually, eliminate, we have them where we want them.

In earlier times, there were one or two near disasters. The poet Blake nearly blew our cover by writing about 'dark satanic mills'. It took a brilliant, three-pronged initiative by Buttercrambe himself to set the record straight. He began by suggesting to scholars that the words could only be interpreted by reference to Blake's private theology. He followed up by making it known that Blake was mad. As the *coup de grâce*, he instituted annual singing of the words in the Albert Hall to a solemn tune by an all-female audience. It was this work that resulted in Buttercrambe's unprecedented lowering to the dignity of Archtempter.

We have also worked hard to ridicule the whole concept of sin. To ninety-nine out of every hundred humans, the word means sexual activity. This interpretation has been fostered by the managers of a section of the newspaper industry which exists solely on its hypocritical exploitation. (For these, our designers have produced a standard page make-up in which a large picture of a nearly-naked woman is juxtaposed with reports about a married vicar having a relationship with a parishioner and a minor member of the Royal Family swimming with their public relations consultant. The stories are written by members of our staff and syndicated worldwide.) That sin covers every aspect of human activity is a fact we have successfully buried.

Recently the Infernal College of Mismanagement (ICM) used some of its first-year students to carry out a survey of managers' views on sin. The results were gratifying, if highly predictable. When asked whether they regarded themselves, their subordinates, their colleagues, their customers or their boss as the most sinful, the response was:

Q: *'Who of the following do you regard as the most sinful?*

– bosses	1,909
– subordinates	994
– colleagues	904
– customers	901
– themselves	4
– don't know	19

Scrutiny of the survey has suggested that three of the four papers suggesting that the manager himself was more sinful were so completed in error. The fourth was probably filled in by a trainee.

The survey also asked managers to suggest what actions they considered most sinful. The combined listing was:

Q: *Please tick those of the following actions you regard as sinful (tick three only)*

Action	*Number ticked*
polluting the environment	5
cheating customers	6
fiddling expenses	9
being found out fiddling expenses	1,741
going home before boss	1,840
lateness at boss's meetings	1,877
disagreeing with boss	1,878

Buckden does not yet fit this. The aim of your labours, is, therefore, to ensure that he does. The commission of any one of the Seven Deadly Sins will ensure Buckden's damnation. However, as you have now been put on the latest Productivity Bonus Scheme, it is in your interest to ensure that Buckden commits as many as possible. I shall take you through each sin separately, and indicate how you can best ensure he commits it.

I will now indoctrinate you into the first of the Seven Deadly Sins of Management – *The Sin of Trendiness*.

Managers are not known outside their sordid, closed little world as fashionable people. Indeed, the juxtaposition of the words 'manager' and 'trendy' may seem, at first sight, grotesque. The idea of a manager prancing down a catwalk or figuring on the cover of a glossy magazine in the latest Italian power suit is laughable. But do not be deceived; managers are neurotically anxious to be in fashion. Naturally they do not use the word. They use such phrases as 'the cutting edge', 'the leading edge', or perhaps 'the state of the art'. But whatever description they use, they will mean 'in the latest fashion'.

This obsession shows itself in many areas, including:

- ideas
- terminology
- health and safety
- toys

I will now explain the application of each to you.

Ideas: here, again, you will sense an apparently basic contradiction. That managers should be described as people of ideas sounds preposterous. They are certainly neither intellectuals nor idealists; indeed, as a race they deeply despise both.

For a large part of human history, this was as far as the matter got, but somewhere about the middle of the last century, the ICM sensed that the moment had come for a change. The increase in economic activity (the 'Industrial

Revolution' as we taught them to call it) had provided a much increased scope for purely intellectual confusion, which we had been a little slow to exploit. A new department of Management Intellectual Confusion (MIC) was established, with two Chairs, of Political Confusion and Moral Confusion respectively.

The first professor of Political Confusion, Souldrop, concentrated on creating a new political philosophy, which he ultimately called 'communism'. As you will have learnt in your first year at ICM, this placed managerial activity at the centre of human affairs. Religious belief, cultural activities and the bonds of human love, were to be replaced by the all-embracing worship of industrial production. Souldrop's PR boys produced the brilliant logo – the 'Hammer and Sickle' that so superbly encapsulated this belief. The whole of society became subservient to making things. The managerial role under this system was reduced to production supervisor. Coal and ore were mined opencast in Siberia to produce heavy plant and machinery which were used to make tractors which were used to grow beans which were fed to cows whose beef fed men who built tanks that were used to intimidate workers to dig ever more coal and ore. When so many tanks were produced they outnumbered the workers they were meant to intimidate, the surplus was used to fill the exhausted coal and ore mines.

The first professor of Moral Confusion was Borehamwood. Sadly, he misinterpreted his brief, his tenure was annulled and he was sent for fundamental reprogramming. He was succeeded by Ampthill, who was immediately successful. His hypothesis was that managers had hitherto been simple people, who had left moral issues to their religious advisers. If, in their pursuit of profit and self-interest, they had wanted someone to do something, they had asked them to do it. If it had not been done, immediately and to their satisfaction, they had sacked the individual concerned, and asked someone else. Ampthill put an end to this. He brought managers to realize that their status was that of mere tradesmen – little more than hewers of wood and drawers of water. He pointed out that no university recognized management as even a subsidiary subject to pad out the first year of a degree course in such essential disciplines as Anglo-Saxon or palaeontology. He thus persuaded managers that they must, to rise in the social hierarchy, demonstrate that their work was based, not, as they had hitherto believed, on getting a job done, but on a framework of complex theory. The discipline of 'Scientific Management' was born.

The fact that this was almost immediately demonstrated to be total nonsense was of no consequence. Ampthill found the USA to be the soft underbelly of the academic world, where management could be introduced as a 'subject' to be talked about almost in the same breath as ancient Greek literature, marine biology and political philosophy. The 'management thinker' (a contradiction in terms, if ever there was one) arose, and soon afterwards the first Graduate School in Business Administration. Naturally it was over half a century and two world wars before even his dedication could gain a foothold in Britain. It goes without saying that the strongest resistance was put up by two unimportant cities in the Midlands of England whose names I forget. The subsequent raising of management theory to a pinnacle of respectability has been a comparatively simple task. The proportion of GNP devoted to its pursuit has risen in inverse proportion to managerial effectiveness.

Much of this growth of management theory has been achieved (as was the rise of communism) by the use of slogans. Most slogans will bear a wide range of 'meanings', and Ampthill for long sought the all-purpose slogan. After many only partially satisfactory attempts, his latest appears to have much more potential. You will have met it already: 'Back to Basics'. Ampthill's original intention was that the slogan should be used by managers; he had envisaged it as a replacement for 'Total Quality Management', a slogan which he intended to promulgate for a party political manifesto. Unfortunately there was a leak in his Private Office, and the all-embracing absence of identifiable meaning of 'Back to Basics' was immediately accepted by the then current public relations advisers of a national party (who are, of course responsible for that party's 'policy-making'). Ampthill had then to make the best of what seemed to be a bad job, although 'Total Quality Management (TQM)' has, it seems to me, continued to do quite well as a management slogan. It has made the fortunes of a large number of consultants, filled awkward gaps in the syllabuses of numerous colleges and business schools, and occupied many thousands of hours of time that would otherwise have been put to productive use. Above all, it has provided first-rate 'thought-replacement therapy' for managers who, without it, would have had to get to grips with real problems.

Ampthill has done much to recoup the situation by his invention of the concept of the quality standard, as embodied in BS5750, ISO9000 and the like. These superb weapons will, when once adopted, ensure the slow and complete strangulation of any organization except, of course, those of the consultants growing fat on showing how the standards must be introduced.

Terminology: words are the most fashion-laden element in human life. They pass in and out of vogue frequently and quickly, and the fashion-conscious humans must ensure they keep fully up-to-date. The process is master-minded by the great Buttercrambe, Dean of Miscommunication Studies at the ICM, and some of the most brilliant brains in the Lowerarchy have been engaged on the task. I myself spent two and a half years during the formative period of my career. Indeed, Tempters who are not members of MINSA (the Mental Institution for Nondescript, Self-centred Asses) would not even be considered for this.

Some of the work may appear fairly humdrum. There is a continuing need for trendy words, expressions and even abbreviations which convey the impression that the user is up-to-the-minute and thus, by an obvious but illogical step, a leader in their field. Such words and phrases may be completely meaningless or capable of an infinite range of meaning. Their meaning is never challenged in use, as to do so would imply that the hearer was *not* up-to-the-minute or a leader, so it hardly matters. The words are the passing favourites of careless and unthinking masters, and can be locked away and forgotten as soon as their novelty has worn off.

ICM does not issue a thesaurus of such expressions in hard copy, as its shelf-life would be too short. It may be purchased on CDROM (although this may be beyond your pocket) or accessed on-line. Examples are likely to be outdated before you receive them, but I will nevertheless let you see a few from the current list, to give the flavour:

the adaptive organization (watch for the stable organization . . .)
benchmarking
best practice
champion
change agent (detergent comes next)
cross-functional co-ordination, integration, etc
delayering (redelayering is about to be included)
empowerment
facilitation
global . . . (what follows does not matter)
integrated intra-firm activities
interface capabilities
intrapreneur
leading edge

lean manufacturing
learning organization
learning outcome
multi-disciplinary team
multiskilling
outplacement
outsourcing (insourcing comes next)
re-engineering
relayering (derelayering is about to be included)
self-directed work teams
serendipity
synergy, synergistic

You will be well aware of the latest, and one of the most glorious of all Buttercrambe's initiatives, known on Earth as PC (Political Correctness). It is based, as all the very best attacks are, on something of real benefit to the human race. There is no question, and never has been, that words matter; it has been Buttercrambe's genius to make them matter too much, and in the wrong way.

There are six phases to PC. They are:

Phase one Take a word that is entirely innocent, and of clear meaning, such as 'Popsie'. The word Popsie is derived from poppa, meaning a doll – the same word as a puppet. It thus means a small person capable of giving delight to others; no harm could be meant.

Phase two The word is loaded with insulting overtones. Popsie becomes a word meaning a female created to provide pleasure for the dominant male.

Phase three An alternative, politically correct, word is substituted, which carries no insulting overtones. The popsie is called a woman. This is factual, and devoid of blame.

Phase four The alternative word is loaded with innuendo, especially in the eyes of those so called. Yet others are found to purge this slur. Now, the real characteristic of the individual is hidden; humans have moved a further step away from reality. To avoid discrimination the woman is called a 'person'. It is forgotten that men, boys, girls and trans-sexuals are also people.

Phase five The new words are gradually seen as pejorative, and are replaced by yet broader generalizations. This phase is still under development, but Buttercrambe has it in mind to initiate use of the word 'humankind'.

Phase six 'Humankind' will be replaced by 'lifeforms'. In due course, this will finally be replaced by 'things', or if this is also felt to be discriminatory, by 'ug'.

Thus, in six simple stages, language that has taken many thousands of years to refine, and which has rightly been regarded as the crowning achievement of the human race, will be progressively 'de-constructed'.

There are some amongst the Lowerarchy who believe that Buttercrambe has overreached himself with this project. I must admit to some doubts, but far fewer than I had only a year or two ago. In this time, he has ensured that coffee cannot be safely described as 'black', that 'ballcocks' must be described as 'spherical floating-arm fluid-control emission equipment'. Fat men he has designated 'other-sized individuals', thus laying the groundwork for rivalry between them and thin men, thin women, tall men, tall women, short men and short women during the next phase. I am now inclined to believe that Buttercrambe's outrageous project will succeed.

Health and safety: we have put managers under pressure from another angle in this area. Fashionable diseases are an old ploy, but it was only thanks to the unconventional genius of Fotheringay that they have been adapted to the situation of today's executive.

His first attempts were unoriginal; in the earlier years of the present century, he spent much effort in applying the 'Peptic Ulcer' myth into management. It would be unjust to claim that he had no success. On the contrary, there was a time when any self-respecting senior executive who claimed he was not suffering ulcers would be looked at askance by colleagues and passed over for vacancies, on the grounds that he could not be pulling his weight.

Fotheringay's next attempt was also time-worn. Under the slogan 'Breathalyse your Boss' he developed an initiative to draw attention to drink as an occupational hazard for managers. He was treading a fine line here. The temptation to alcoholic excess is, and will remain, one of our more powerful weapons against managers as against others; you will have been shown the ovensful of executive sots 'drying out' in the deeper cellars of ICM. None the less, Fotheringay has had measurable success in making managers feel guilty for totally harmless levels of alcohol intake. The executive cocktail cabinet and the pre-lunch sherry in the executive dining room are now things of the past. When offered a drink, the executive fresh from his MBA will ask for a Malvern Water or a diet Coke; only the few in their middle age not yet declared redundant would still dare to ask for a G & T.

The balance of advantages from this initiative is still to be fully assessed, but a recent study does give some support to Fotheringay's contention that the scope for raising guilt outweighs any enhancement of post-prandial thinking.

However this initiative is finally judged, there can be no doubt that the experience gained is now being put to effective use. Fotheringay's team have recently been working on a range of highly imaginative new conditions. The first to gain credibility was 'Repetitive Strain Injury' (RSI). The suggestion that the human body is ill-adapted to repeated activity seemed to some to be too far-fetched. The scoffers made jokes – some of them lewd - about many forms of repetitive action that caused no injury.

All seemed lost until, as so often, the computer came to their aid. The breakthrough was made when, with the help of one of our tame trade unions, the concept was applied to keyboard operators. That a foolhardy judge attempted to stand out against us is of no importance at all. On the contrary, the resulting confusion has only added to the fun.

Fotheringay's next initiative – the 'Sick Building Syndrome – really seems to many to be going too far. Even our trade union agents have expressed doubts. I alone amongst his colleagues remain certain of its potential. The concept that a building can be capable of damaging the health of those working in it elegantly links the modern belief in the wicked and uncaring boss with the primaeval belief in the haunted house. It must be a winner.

Try a few ideas on the Staff Representative in the United Group HQ building. When, for example, were the water tanks last checked for Legionnaires' Diseases? Are there overhead electric cables, a nearby substation, or other producers of electro-magnetic fields? Do trains carrying nuclear waste pass nearby? How about radon gas? Was blue asbestos used to lag the pipework in the Executive

Washroom? Does the number of VDUs per square metre of window area exceed the maximum permitted by the Health and Safety Executive? Microwaves escaping from the recently-installed oven in the canteen may well be penetrating into the Customer Service Department. Does the increasing use of mobile phones generate ozone? Might the plastic from which the venetian blinds are made degenerate into a powder that produces impotence when inhaled? Does the static electricity generated by friction between Production and Sales cause nausea in Accounts? Certainly the Chief Commissionaire swears the disembodied shape of a Victorian shareholder floats up the main staircase nearly every day soon after he returns from the Pig and Whistle.

Following these successes, Fotheringay's team has been funded to work on a number of projects. These include Administrator's Ankle, Boardroom Belly, Comptroller's Crutch, Director's Digit, Executive's Elbow, Foreman's Finger, Gaffer's Gut, Manager's Mouth, and Proprietor's Palm. The concept behind most of these is fairly obvious. One or two, however, display true Fotheringay originality.

Comptroller's Crutch, for example, is a condition we are promoting actively amongst company accountants. It has not hitherto been generally recognized that accountants are hypochondriac, and Fotheringay is convinced he has identified a gap in the market for occupational diseases. Research under hypnosis showed that organizational accountants have a secret fear of rejection. This was first suspected when an increasing number were observed to be using the grandiose title of 'comptroller', implying that they, and they alone, held decision-making power. The archaic form of the word also clearly indicated a crude attempt to cloak their arrogance with spurious respectability.

In fact, the typical accountant is a loner desperately

striving for acceptance from his colleagues. He hides in a maze of incomprehensible figures and meaningless jargon because he cannot face the uncomfortable realities and complex relationships of the real world. In earlier times, he would have taken refuge in the nearest monastery (or convent, depending on orientation). In place of their never-ending battle with the absurdities of our friends the Inland Revenue, they would have struggled with the finer points of theology, such as the number of Archangels capable of dancing on the point of a needle. Instead of currying the favour of their paymasters through creative accounting, they would have offered to say masses for their souls. It is no coincidence that the financial year begins at Easter, or that the traditional time for presenting national budgets was during Lent. Fotheringay has listed no less than fifteen similarities between the method of calculating tax allowances and that for selecting the collects for Evening Prayer.

On this basis, it became clear that the vulnerability of accountants could be exploited. Fotheringay identified their habit of sitting on fences during boardroom battles, and promoted the belief that it was damaging to a particularly delicate part of their anatomy. This has now been officially recognized by two professional accountancy institutions, and the number of days sickness taken by accountants has more than doubled.

Director's Digit is a condition that has not yet gained official recognition. It is based on the supposed propensity of directors to point accusing fingers at those of their number they wish to unseat. In fact, there is little evidence that this occurs, as directors engaged in discrediting a colleague invariably hide their intentions behind warm handshakes and friendly smiles. I fear Fotheringay may have to rethink this one.

He is on much firmer ground with *Executive's Elbow*. No senior manager could succeed without the ability to elbow his or her rivals out of the way. This is true both literally and figuratively. Literal demonstrations of this ability are visible at any buffet or reception attended by senior managers, although close observation is necessary; the cleverer the executives, the less obvious are their manoeuvres to get at the caviar canapés or the smoked salmon sandwiches before their rivals.

Figurative elbowing of colleagues is a basic management skill, and you will recollect (I hope) the advice I gave during your earlier struggles with Buckden.

Perhaps the longest-lasting and most successful of Fotheringay's initiatives is the promotion of *management stress*. That managers, whose role offers excellent working conditions, satisfying work, wide freedom of action, high rewards, acknowledged status, continual variety, and attractive prospects should be victims of chronic stress stretches credibility to its limits.

Only a genius of Fotheringay's calibre could achieve such a coup. But by funding carefully-targeted research on heart disease, smoking, drinking, drug-taking, sexual inadequacy and marital breakdown, he has built up and reinforced the picture of the piteous plight of senior executives. His clever approach to cholesterol is typical. By devising a simple method of measurement, he has focused attention, raised anxiety and created an industry with a new set of vested interests. That the connection between all this and illness may be complex and unproven he has kept carefully hidden. The day when valetudinarian executives spend more time in the clinic and on the occupational counsellor's couch than in the Boardroom is not far off.

Fear of illness generates the desire to maintain health. Some excellent work has been done here also, and we are having success in encouraging distressed managers to turn to transcendental meditation, massage therapy, and a range of other exciting developments.

Sound therapy is a current interest. Whilst arranging a

reverse takeover, for example, or planning the next round of redundancies, executives now have the choice of tapes of Mozart, the dawn chorus, waves breaking on the shore, wind breaking in a number 73 bus-queue, nightingales in a Surrey wood, a pair of dolphins engaged in a bitter domestic argument, or perhaps a table being laid for a large meal.

Aroma therapy is also breaking new ground. We are promulgating the belief that budget planning can be made more effective if undertaken in an office scented by the briar rose; product development can be helped by the fragrance of new-mown hay; appraisals go more smoothly when conducted in the aroma of frying kippers; project meetings are different if conducted to the smell of rotting compost, and termination interviews are more enjoyable when accompanied by a strong whiff of burning rubber.

Toys: you should enjoy playing with the Executive Toys currently under development in the ICM laboratories. Older designs, such as suspended metal balls that slapped into each other, and fighting matchstick figures, lacked clarity of purpose. The growth of electronics has widened the scope enormously, and toys such as electronic organizers, beepers and portable telephones have broken entirely new ground. New microchips have kept up the pace, and some really exciting developments are now under way.

The most promising, I think, is the All-Purpose Electronic Micro-Universe (APEMU). The idea was sparked off by Gulval's All-Purpose Boy Scout's pen-knife. It would not be correct to claim that APEMU will cover every need in an executive's life, but it covers many of the commonest. APEMU is indistinguishable externally from the normal briefcase. When opened, it reveals a fully-integrated package including dictaphone, computer, telephone, fax, personal organizer, biorhythm indicator, breathalyser, hygrometer, sphygmometer, aspectarian, talking timetable for the Trans-Siberian Railway, and water detector. The Mark II will include a device for removing stones from horses hooves.

Overall, I think the sin of Trendiness will offer the ideal opportunity to drive Buckden into our grasp. Which aspect you find most helpful, I am content to leave to your rapidly developing judgement. However, I would direct your attention to the difficulties we are already making for him in the United Group. I can see two possibilities. Suggest first that United's range of products are outdated. Persuade him that he should replace the traditional designs with his own, up-to-the-minute, modern patterns. Ensure that he does no market research, and accepts no advice from his own marketing professionals; if necessary, let him sack the whole department.

Second, try the Total Quality Management approach, and confuse this in Buckden's mind with the BS5750 standard. As a younger man, I doubt whether he would have been silly enough to fall for such vague, modern rubbish, but point out to him that contracts for gnomes to decorate public parks and local government offices will be placed with other firms unless he obtains BS5750 accreditation. Hint that rivals are on the verge of obtaining accreditation. There may be difficulty in finding an agency with scope for the accreditation of gnome manufacture, but I am sure you can find a way round this one. Have a word with one or two of your middle-aged, outplaced managers; I am sure they would love to become quality consultants.

I have heard from the Watchers that a potential competitor to United Group – International Crafts Consolidated (ICC) – has emerged in the market. The Chief Executive, is young and lives a life-style of the most blatant sinfulness. He has, however, by virtue of his ability to make money at a rate not equalled since the election of Prime Minister Thatcher, already been accepted as a member of the Great and Good, a fact which Buckden has noted with disguised horror. Find out more about this man and his organization at once; we must put him to good use.

Keep me in the picture.

Your ever-loving Uncle

Barripper

Instrument 1: TRENDINESS

(NB This Instrument may only be used by Tempters who are corporate members of the Infernal Institute of Psychometrics (IIP) and have completed the appropriate five-week training seminar.)

INSTRUCTIONS

This is not a test. There are no right or wrong answers, although your whole future will depend on how you complete it. Just work out what we think is the most balanced reply and hope for the best.

Choose ONLY 5 of the following statements which are important to you; reject the other 5 out of hand.

1. Collecting rare paintings implies the availability of appropriate storage space.
2. Compulsory dress suits at VIP functions are anachronistic.
3. Political correctness has gone too far.
4. Saturday afternoon sport is a sublimation of man's aggressive instincts.
5. The road to Mandalay is riddled with pitfalls.
6. Conditions can change very rapidly when you're in the garden.
7. The embarrassment of others is more embarrassing than my own.
8. The world stage is no longer what it was.

9. Television has too dominant an influence on the old.
10. Mandarin oranges should be available all year round.

SCORING

1. No, no, ten times no. If so, so what? Score 0
2. Untrue. They remain a benchmark for a bygone age. Score 0
3. Not yet; hopefully there's more fun to come. Score 0
4. True, but what else might they get up to? Score 0
5. More perilous than you think, but where is Mandalay? Score 10
6. Hidden depth. Shows flexibility to rapid change. Score 10
7. Evidence of lack of control. Score 0
8. An historical perspective will stand you in good stead. Score 10
9. Yes, and the cause of all the trouble. Score 10
10. No, they would lose their appeal. Score 0

ANALYSIS

40: your capacity for picking a winner is faultless. Try your hand at inventing your own trends; you can't go wrong.

30: you have a penchant for following fashion however unthinking it may be. You will go far and it will drag you low.

20: you show signs of dangerously perceptive insight. Can none the less come a cropper by picking the wrong options. Often feel that you've just missed the boat.

10: you do miss the boat quite regularly but the damage

you wreak is always controlled. A sitter on the fence, safety first is your motto. Others will lead and you will be pulled along.

0: the world is just passing you by; unphased by current affairs and events, you blunder blindly on regardless. No sensitivity whatsoever. Should have a happy life.

Chapter 2

Conceit

'He is a self-made man, and worships his creator.'

JOHN BRIGHT

My dear Relubbus

I am delighted with your first report. That Buckden should insist on accreditation under the BS5750 Quality Standard for the entire Group as the top priority will prove a major element in his final overthrow. Equally powerful is his proposed sweeping away of the traditional range of gnomes, and sacking of the entire staff of both marketing and design departments. Now we will not only have him but his company too. Already the Watchers report that his senior managers are meeting in secret groups to question what can be done.

You may also already have seen the Watchers' excellent report on Buckden's competitor, International Crafts Consolidated (ICC). If so, you will have noted how ICC started by attempting to copy United's gnomes. They invested a large amount of money on a mad biotechnologist who claimed to have developed a technique for cloning plastics, and produced an imitation of United's best selling line they wittily called the 'G-Gnome'. It was over a year before they realized that the biotechnologist was a fraud, and that the 'cloned' gnomes were cast in his potting shed, using a stolen United mould. Now, however, ICC's lower-priced products have taken off in the recession and they are buying up out-of-town property to open a chain of new garden centres which will, naturally, stock only their own range of gnomes. According to the Watchers, Buckden at last sees them as a threat. You should have already discovered that the founder/chairman of ICC is called Smithers. Familiarize yourself with his file immediately.

The second of the Seven Deadly Sins of Management is *The Sin of Conceit.*

It is impossible to be a successful manager without believing you are better than others, and that you deserve a higher place and greater rewards. Sadly, there are a few who combine self-confidence with a desire to use any superior gifts they have for the general good – of their subordinates, their organization and society as a whole – in the same way that a few rich humans use their wealth. Luckily for us this category is very small, and Buckden does not belong to it.

There are Five Ages of executive conceit:

- ambition
- arrogance
- infallibility
- ISO
- CCG

Ambition is often regarded as a Good Thing in the young. The classic examples of this are to be found amongst recently recruited graduates. Most trainee Tempters are given one or two assignments of this type during their early programming. A degree of success is almost certain, even for the most inexperienced and least talented of trainees, the risks of failure are slight, and there is plenty of time to recover from them.

We invented the Graduate Traineeship many years ago. Its aims were simple. It reinforced the new graduate's belief in his or her innate superiority and the certainty of their rapid rise to the top. It ensured that other employees would regard them with a destructive mixture of fear, jealousy, amusement and loathing. New graduates become impatient if promotion is not continuous and rapid. They will be unable to tolerate the repetitive grind necessary to achieve results in any worthwhile job, and look for immediate results. They will expect to be moved upwards before properly learning any job, before achieving any measurable and worthwhile results, and, above all, before their mistakes catch up with them.

From this base, Droomer of the Graduate Recruitment Directorate has made immense progress. For some time now, he has worked towards the objective of ensuring a university education for all. The arguments so originally and brilliantly detailed by Droomer to support his strategy are that it makes for social equality, eliminates élitism and allows young people several years of irresponsibility during which they are vulnerable to almost every temptation we can devise. These arguments are irresistible to politicians; to say that they support 'better education and training' is an automatic vote winner, and to resist such a policy is out of the question. The strategy also ensures continuing expansion of the education sector. Working from our base in the University of Pinner, Droomer has turned many prominent members of this group.

The future looks fascinating. A continually increasing proportion of national resources will be consumed by education. Those resources will be progressively diminished by the loss of productive effort from those being educated. A continuing stream of new subjects of study will have to be devised to meet the needs of the capabilities of those requiring university education. Three years of hedonistic socializing and unfounded self-belief are capped by the award of Honours in Film Studies or a BA in Long Jump and Media Research. The job expectations of the increasing army of graduates will be impossible to meet. In due

course, when all have first degrees, the whole process can be moved forward to higher levels; Droomer looks for the day when the lowest acceptable qualification for part-time waiter/waitress is at MBA level.

I have digressed, but the foundations of executive conceit are best laid during this first Age. The standard technique is to make new graduates believe that they were God's gift to whatever organization had been fortunate enough to recruit them. (We have taught humans to use 'God's gift' as a term of sarcastic appreciation.) They must see the many mistakes that are being made by existing staff, and the many opportunities that are being missed. From this, they must be led to regard those around them as of inferior mental capacity and in urgent need of guidance. They will in any case have been trained to believe that intelligence is the only requisite for problem solving, and will naturally despise those who do not share the same view. They will also find it difficult to hide their feelings, as they will have received no training in the political skills that we know make the difference between success and failure. They will give dogmatic and uncalled-for advice to those who have struggled for years with intractable difficulties. They will rapidly use up the capital of goodwill given to the young and inexperienced. With effective tradecraft, this process will be accompanied by increasing ill-will on both sides.

This did not happen to Buckden, thanks to your failures. He has for this reason been slow to develop in the second Age; that of arrogance.

Executive arrogance seems so natural that there is little that needs saying about it. Few managers in mid career do not believe that they rule by divine right, that their superiority is beyond question, and that it must be willingly accepted by their subordinates. However, in recent years we have, due to some extremely slack work by the HRD Directorate of the MDU, come under pressure in this crucial area. A school of management has been allowed to grow up which uses jargon such as 'democratic decision-making', 'facilitation', and 'empowerment'. The concept of managers who really believe their role is to help rather than command is, of course, virtually incredible, but we have established a project team of some of our most experienced Tempters to ensure that we do not lose control of the situation. Using the research facilities of ICM's Centre of Mediocrity at the University of Pinner as a base, they have developed a Code of Worst Practise known as the Executive's Little Red Book. The Code is a very thorough document, which you must study in detail. Here are one or two dicta from it:

1 As managers you are always and in all ways superior to those you manage; that is how you got your job.

2 To err is not only human, but the hallmark of top

managers. The only unforgivable error is to be found out.

34 The golden rule in selecting staff: choose only those who are less skilled than you.

55 Always listen carefully to what subordinates say to you; you might learn something which could be used in evidence against them.

74 In all things ensure: I get the credit; they get the blame.

406 All instructions must be sufficiently ambiguous to ensure you can avoid blame in case of failure.

1007 Only give palpably insincere thanks.

1678 A subordinate who displays superior skills to your own must be immediately either promoted into someone else's department or sacked.

It is possible to obtain the full Code on cassette. I strongly recommend you to purchase this and use it for Buckden's subliminal indoctrination. Adaptors to mobile phones are now available for this purpose, although the present design only works inside the M25 (except for deafening static near Heathrow).

Buckden is now on the verge of the third age; that of **infallibility**. It is your task to ensure that his infallibility rivals that of the Bishop of Rome. The process of ageing that is unavoidable for humans ensures that most managers come to believe in their infallibility without further help from us. Each day during which their whims are treated as gospel reinforces the conviction; each stage of promotion lessens the number of those in a position to challenge them.

It is sometimes asked how the many managers who have spent much of their career making mistakes can be seduced into a feeling of infallibility. There are two answers to this. Those silly enough to make mistakes that are found out are already within our clutches; the joys of delayering, outplacement, and outsourcing are only the start of the fate that awaits them. But the doom of those whose mistakes are hidden is even more certain, although it may be delayed. Civil servants and local government officers, for example, whose promotion continues unabated whilst others suffer from their incompetence often believe they have escaped our grasp – but they have not. One by one we drag them off, filling their places on the Committees, Commissions, Councils, Boards and Authorities with life-sized holograms.

Of course the most fruitful area for fostering the Sin of Conceit amongst executives of all kinds is, in Britain, the Honours System. This is something we have worked on tirelessly for several centuries, and of which the Arch-tempter in charge – Borrowdale – is rightly proud. His only failures, which he freely admits, are in transplanting the system into other countries and failing to hide the contradiction of 'a classless honours system' from all but the politicians who have the responsibility of manipulating it for their own ends. I suspect that, despite his engaging honesty on these points, notice will eventually be taken of this deficiency, and the inevitable outplacement will occur. What this may do to the career prospects of Senior Tempters remains to be seen, but I live in hope.

In the meantime, as Buckden is a British Chief Executive (CE), the Honours System must remain one of the very strongest weapons in your armoury. As I have already pointed out, he has for some time become progressively more obsessed with obtaining an honour. It has started to affect his work in a number of ways, and you must exploit and add to these. However, before looking at these in detail, I must brief you on some aspects of the system as a whole.

Borrowdale designed the system (for it was designed) to meet three objectives. The first was to assist trainee toast-masters, the second to ensure the industrial downfall of Britain, and the third to provide amusement for the rest of the world. It is to the second of these I must draw your attention. Borrowdale's system operates to harm Britain in several ways. By giving high 'honours' to civil servants, it ensures that their stranglehold on the productive and creative elements in society is preserved and that a distorted scale of contributions to society is created and maintained. But it is the effect on senior executives of the slowly approaching vision of an 'honour' which has most value to us. This vision goads them and their partners and causes fundamental behavioural changes. Senior executives who previously had time only for their business will suddenly discover that they can spare time to sit on the bench (as the comfortably upholstered judges' seats in subordinate courts are quaintly known) or one or two public bodies. Those who have hitherto let their reputation look after itself will engage the services of expensive PR consultants. Many will suddenly feel the need to contribute, or rather to ensure that their organization contributes, to the funds of whichever party seems likely to win the next election. The rebels who have for long openly criticized government policies will suddenly start to support every passing political fashion. Most amusingly, you will see those who have throughout their life thought of nothing but their own well-being developing a public commitment to a Charity or Good Cause.

Borrowdale is developing a special range of honours suitable for executives and managers. Whilst this is not yet approved by Council, I can list some of what seem likely to be the most useful. These include:

MBE	Member of the Boardroom Elite
KLK	Knight of the Long Knives
CGB	Companion of the Golden Bedsocks
OMI	Order of Managerial Incompetence
CDE	Chief Destroyer of the Environment
OJ	Member of the Most Noble Order of the Jacuzzi

The whole fabric is a key element in the self-admiration club of the 'Great and Good' to which I referred in my last letter. There is, incidentally, a distinction between this group and the 'Establishment'. The 'Great and Good' are those who are used to fill the public committees, commissions, boards, councils, authorities, and quangos that I have already mentioned. They see themselves as important, but in fact wield no power worth mentioning. The 'Establishment', on the other hand, are those who do have power (subject, of course, to our overall control). This group consists of a few senior politicians and civil servants, and assorted academics, media owners and top executives and entrepreneurs. There is also the recent coinage – 'the Chattering Classes'. This is a self-congratulatory term for self-styled intellectuals who may or may not also be 'Great and Good' or 'Establishment'. It has come into being because for the British, the term 'intellectual' is unusable. To avoid misunderstanding, I strongly recommend the use of the generic term on which you will hear more: the Golden Gravy Train (GGT).

There has been much talk over the years about the essential outward symbols of managerial conceit, executive status symbols, and I know you received full training in this subject during your studies at ICM. One of the key aspects, as you will know, is that most symbols have a limited life. Even the executive suit – the coat that matches the trousers – is under challenge in those organizations that have been bought out by the Japanese. It is therefore essential for Tempters to keep their knowledge fully up-to-date;

this is one of the many areas in which Continuing Professional Development (CPD) is a must. The following are some of the executive status symbols due for launch during the coming year.

- Colour videophone
- Alderney-registered car
- Vegan executive lunches
- Company flat in Tooting Bec
- Transvestite male secretary
- Open-air board meetings
- Chairless office
- Son busking at Oxford Circus tube station

You must obtain the full list from the ICM Publications Department.

I mentioned earlier the use of PR consultants by those CEs who are aiming for honours. The MDU has now established its own PR consultancy, with the twin objectives of helping towards the long-term discrediting of some of our trickier subjects and turning a quick buck.

The scope is wide. We shall arrange speaking engagements for our clients; the presentation of prestigious lectures and papers and speeches at conferences and Annual Dinners. Virtually all CEs are, of course, incapable of either writing or delivering a speech. We shall therefore offer an expert speech writing service based on their requirements for texts that are illogical, pompous, self-congratulatory and boring. This will give them the ego trips they seek, whilst helping in the destruction of their credibility.

We shall also help our clients to obtain nomination for medals and awards. There are already a number of these available for CEs; it is our aim to establish new ones. Present plans include:

- The Gold Medal for Services to Tax Evasion

- The Electric Bicycle Award for the worst-selling product
- The Asset Stripper of the Year Award
- The Silver Axe for Executive Redundancy
- The Hostile Takeover Challenge Cup

A service will be offered for CEs' 'How-I-did-it' autobiographies. We have already set up a panel of ghost writers, as few CEs are capable of stringing three words together. (Unfortunately, this service does have the considerable difficulty of ensuring such books are published before the subject's business fails or they are arrested on charges of financial impropriety.)

It was proposed to establish a division to help CEs who wish to become TV personalities, but few have been willing to grow the necessary whiskers, and none so far have shown any detectable personality.

And so to the fourth Age of Conceit. Clobham has called this **ISO** or Implications of Strategic Omission. Clobham advises caution. For this age, timing is all and your judgement must be razor sharp. Let me give you a digest of Clobham's artistry.

While Buckden is encouraged to parade his prowess in public with invitations to back-slapping dinners and nominations for the odd non-executive directorship, there comes a time, quite simply, when the invitations fail to arrive – but only irregularly, almost by oversight; in fact, by strategic omission. The belief that his name is being spread throughout the land will make his ballooning ego crave for more. *That* is the moment to strike – the moment at which his name is omitted from the list of those invited to join this committee, that board, this conference, that dinner. He will overlook being left out once, but twice will give him cause for reflection; the third time will see him suffering the fear of being sidelined, the cold of omission. He will wonder if a wind of change is affecting his fortunes. He will adopt a corporate approach to his festering insecurity and outwardly feign relief at the release of pressure on his invaluable time. Next he may claim that United Group is being slighted. He might go as far as to say that the future of United is at risk. Inwardly he will be assailed by doubts. Of course, we, and everyone else, will recognize that his ego needs peer acclaim like a drug, and condemn his behaviour as conceited fantasy of an irretrievable nature. The seed of destruction will be equally irretrievably sown.

There is a fifth Age to the process of destruction by conceit, although it is rarely reached. However, Buckden has proved resilient in the past and you may well need to implement what Clobham rather conceitedly called **CCG**, or Clobham's Crowning Glory.

CCG is a direct sequitur to the fourth Age. Again it requires split-second timing. CCG consists quite simply in restarting the flow of invitations, but at a lower level. Instead of the Committee for Economic Development, Buckden should receive an invitation to address the Young Wives of Saffron Walden on how managers choose schools for their children; instead of the Council for Research into Regional Developments, Buckden should be asked to talk to the Senior Citizens Thursday Club of Nether Stowey on the importance of dress sense in the young executive; instead of the European Committee for Allocating Grants and Subsidies, Buckden will be invited to address the Young Farmers of Ross-on-Wye on the need for wine lakes in Spain. Nominate him as Governor to the local comprehensive school or second his nomination for the By-pass Committee of the Borough Council. The final twist in Clobham's strategy is that Buckden will be brought low, whilst struggling to maintain prestige and authority. Laughable though it seems, he might even look forward to any recognition that such meaningless little events afford him. He will fight to maintain any semblance of dignity in a domain which will secure his ignominy and oblivion.

There are of course, some more banal tricks to catalyse Buckden's burgeoning arrogance and they too have had noted success in the past. The most celebrated of these is the Reverse Conceit Syndrome (RCS). But use it with care. It has backfired in the past. Reverse Conceit Syndrome argues that the more arrogant the CE becomes, the more he is assailed with events that slight him; the more his conceit grows, the more daily events seem to conspire against his personal grandeur. For example, as Buckden looks forward to the Annual Dinner of his 'Livery Company' – the Worshipful Company of Dustmen and Sewage Artisans (I shall indoctrinate you further about this in a later letter), let it be known that one of his subordinates is invited too. As he scans the Society Pages for mention of his name, drop a letter on his desk haranguing him for his production of defective gnomes and criticizing him for United's quality policy. Let him overhear a conversation where he is referred to whisperingly as a freeloader, or even arrange for his limousine to have a break-down when he has a deadline to meet. The little things often carry the heaviest pain. They certainly burst the biggest bubble of self-esteem.

I also feel sure that it is his desire (and that of his wife) to receive an 'honour' that will prove his Achilles' heel. Several of his acquaintances have already been honoured; two 'got their Ks' in the last Birthday List, and one was created a Life Peer. This is an area in which I am in a position to help you directly. It so happens that I have some little influence with several of the government ministers who advise on these awards. The New Year 'Honours' List is now being drawn up. I will choose a moment in the not too distant future to have a word in the most appropriate ear. I do not think my recommendation will be ignored.

This, then, is the next Sin to which you must tempt Buckden. As you see, there is wide scope. I suspect that the growth of ICC has wounded his personal pride deeply. That any other organization could succeed in the area in which he has done his life's work must be a source of great pain. Work on this, and I think you will find the motivation for much mischief. In addition, find out everything about Smithers' leisure activities, friends and clubs. I suspect Buckden will see him as a rival; from this seed, much evil can grow.

Let us have some more fun here,

Your loving Uncle

Barripper

Instrument 2: CONCEIT

INSTRUCTIONS

The following self-assessment instrument is not to be taken too seriously, nor indeed, too lightly. Do not imagine that the end results are recognizable by others. Merely select one of the options a, b, c or d for each of the ten questions or statements.

1. Do you catch yourself gazing in the mirror

   a) Monday mornings?
   b) too often?
   c) never?
   d) and find someone else looking back?

2. Are you more capable than others

   a) in showing the way forward?
   b) in making and carrying out decisions?
   c) in everything?
   d) in times of crisis?

3. Do you regret the need for delegation

   a) because you can do it better?
   b) because others can do it better?
   c) always?
   d) never?

4. Do you feel that adopting the latest trend is

    a) essential to your corporate image?
    b) a necessary evil?
    c) good to keep 'them' on their toes?
    d) a waste of time?

5. People who call a spade a spade are

    a) distasteful?
    b) lucky to be able to?
    c) to be tolerated?
    d) admirable?

6. Do you bang the drum against

    a) fraud and corruption?
    b) exploitation of the Third World?
    c) the Bank of England?
    d) government policy?

7. If you don't blow your own trumpet

    a) others won't?
    b) others will?
    c) you'll sink without trace?
    d) you'll have to manipulate others to do so?

8. Do you consider yourself above

    a) personal liability?

b) conflicts of interest?

c) public condemnation?

d) a price?

9. Does the end justify the means

a) always?

b) never?

c) sometimes?

d) depends?

10. Is being right

a) a driving force?

b) an excuse?

c) the trump card?

d) a cross you have to bear?

SCORING

1.	a 2	b 7	c 4	d 10
2.	a 5	b 0	c 10	d 3
3.	a 10	b 0	c 5	d 2
4.	a 9	b 1	c 7	d 2
5.	a 9	b 2	c 10	d 0
6.	a 10	b 10	c 3	d 0
7.	a 0	b 10	c 2	d 5
8.	a 10	b 10	c 10	d 10
9.	a 10	b 0	c 2	d 10
10.	a 10	b 4	c 6	d 8

ANALYSIS

65+: many of your actions are pure, almost unconscious. But there is a negative side; your conceit is becoming obvious. Be careful your subordinates haven't got you sussed.

50+: you show promise; you've still got a little way to go but you're well on the way; you probably work too hard at arrogance, and not enough at straightforward pomposity.

Under 30: a disappointment – there's so much hope for you that your self-effacement might see you go totally unnoticed. Be wary that your lack of conceit is not taken for lack of competence.

Chapter 3
Politicking

'My face is pink, my hair is sleek,
I dine at Blenheim once a week.'

ANON

My dear Relubbus

This is the moment we have both been waiting for; celebration is certainly in order. I shall allow myself an extra hour in the torture chamber, and I am prepared to allow you fifteen minutes' sleep tonight. I have already completed my report to the Secretary of the Appointments Panel, indicating the steps I took to achieve this great victory. I also referred briefly to your involvement. From now on, *Sir* Andrew is ours. A recent study confirmed that of those receiving knighthoods or peerages in the last fifty Honours lists 65 per cent were already in our safe keeping, 17 per cent were otherwise committed. (Records of the remaining 18 per cent appeared to have been lost.)

The 'accidental' meeting you arranged between Sir Andrew and Smithers of ICC in the superloo at Euston Station was well done. By such events, empires have been destroyed.

You will appreciate how his new grandeur will strengthen his tendencies to commit the two sins we have already discussed. As a Knight his conceit has been boosted out of all recognition. What you may not yet have realized is the impetus his elevation will give towards the remaining sins. The third Deadly Sin of Management, for example, to which you must now turn your attention, is *The Sin of Politicking*. Buckden has played politics quite skilfully during his career. He would not have reached his present position otherwise. Now, however, in his new role as a Public Figure, we can readily find ways of tempting him to use these skills to the bad. He is not in fact a member of the 'Establishment' (see my last letter to you), but he is more than ever convinced that he should be. From this, two useful possibilities arise; he can be made to believe that he is, and persuaded to overplay his hand; or he can be shown that he is not, and driven to ever more desperate attempts to be accepted. You must remain alert to both. Perhaps more than anything, he will be on the watch to do whatever he can to ensure Smithers does not catch him up in the honours race or – unthinkable thought – overtake him. Play on this nerve.

There are several definitions of 'politics'. One of the most frequently quoted is:

'Politics is the Art of the Possible'

although even Buttercrambe himself has been unable to extract any meaning from the phrase. Commoner and more useful are those which talk of politics in terms of 'string-pulling', 'having friends in high places' and the like. These are well summarized as:

'It's not what you know but whom you know.'

Few managers would disagree with this. Indeed, the concept has been recently repackaged and sanitized by the growing use by managers of the word 'network'.

There is, however, far more to the concept than this. Following his extensive studies, Blatherwyke now defines the true nature of politics as:

'Exploiting desirable emotions to achieve undesirable results.'

This has been accepted as the official definition by the Council of ICM, and it is essential that you understand its implications and the help it can give you in your destruction of Buckden.

Thus, applying the definition to the field of national politics, politicians have had no difficulty in justifying anything from unjust taxation to genocide. The desire to protect society against crime, for example, can be used to inflict torture, wrongful imprisonment and death. The desire to aid the people of developing countries can be used to bolster up their vicious rulers and sell them arms; the desire to house the poor can be used to support armies of bureaucrats and corrupt administrators.

The definition reads across naturally to management. Managers feel comfortable to see themselves as politicians, although this feeling is rarely admitted. Their self-image as 'movers and shakers' implies a knowledge of the motivation of those around them, and the ability to use this knowledge to manipulate.

An understanding of the way in which high-level decisions are made is one of the crucial differences between your work as a Junior Tempter, and the tasks you must master when destroying a CE such as Buckden has now become. The lower human orders, whether in management or any other field, have a blind, childish faith in the integrity and skill of the decision-making processes of those above them. Naturally, we hide the true nature of the processes from them, and they therefore fill the gap by fantasizing. Although they would never admit it, their images are based on pictures of childhood – the child protected by loving, all-knowing parents. This is the only model they have for those with power over them, and their thinking mixes parents, gods and rulers in a confused, cloudy haze. This does not mean that they see everything their rulers do as good and right; just as children fight with their parents, so they will fight with their rulers and believe them to be wrong, unjust, even evil. But it does mean that they believe their rulers to be possessed of magic powers; the foresight, insight and cleverness they themselves lack. If they did not so believe, there would be little basis for the authority they allow to their rulers.

Most never come to realize the actual processes of high-level decision-making. They insist on thinking of those above them as fundamentally honest, intelligent and well-advised. Most cannot understand that their decisions are based on a political process involving self-interest, bluff, blackmail, treachery, threats and deceits. To speak in this context of the 'law of the jungle' is to slander the jungle and all its inhabitants. A human poet got close to it when he spoke of 'ignorant armies' that 'clash by night'. It is the ability first to understand and then to engage successfully in this process that distinguishes those who 'succeed' (in human terms); ie those whom we can best manipulate for our own ends.

CEs must be politicians at two levels; the **internal** (organizational) and the **national** or, as many of them express it, with a small and a big 'p'. I wish to brief you first about the operation of national Politics - politics with a 'big p' – as it affects people like Buckden.

There are Three Principles of all politics:

- To him who shouts the loudest shall be given
- Not in my back yard
- Don't let the mugs find out

At **national** level (the 'Big P') these are applied through a number of mechanisms.:

- Tariffs and quotas
- Subsidies

- Grants
- The Good Cause
- Taxes

I will now explain the most important aspects of these, and consider how you may use them to hasten Buckden's destruction.

Tariffs, quotas and similar methods of restricting international trade can be most useful to us. Like flogging and the death penalty, the idea of restricting competitive imports has an almost irresistible, common-sense appeal. The approach has the added attraction that it is one on which both proprietors and workforce can usually agree. This would be an ideal technique were Buckden's company being ruined by floods of cheap plastic gnomes imported from Iceland, where they were produced by sweated labour. He could then campaign for the imposition of a punitive level of customs duty on imported gnomes to preserve United's market.

Apart from the fact that Iceland is not flooding the market with cheap plastic gnomes, tariffs have serious snags as a weapon of policy. Other industries may depend on their ability to sell to Iceland. They will inevitably suffer when Iceland retaliates for the gnome tax with a swingeing import duty on, for example, refrigerators. The gnome tax may also cause heavy unemployment in Iceland amongst the very section of the population to which United was seeking to sell gnomes. It is also possible that United purchases some of its raw materials from Iceland, and may find duties imposed on these. Whether, therefore, we would be right to hint to Buckden that he should call for tariff changes will always be a matter of the most delicate judgement. This is a matter not for you, but the ICM Policy Sub-Committee. Besides, tariff protection is usually used in a last-ditch attempt to protect dying industries and this is not, yet, true of garden gnomes.

Subsidies are also a highly complex matter. They used to be called the 'Robin Hood' tax, as they are a mechanism for redistributing taxpayers' money from one group to another. However, Yarwell showed that this was a misnomer, as Robin Hood redistributed from the rich, whom he held to ransom, to the deserving poor, whilst subsidies redistribute from the deserving poor to any group capable of holding the government to ransom.

Scorrier has had immense success in this area. His technique is firmly rooted in Buttercrambe's definition of politics; first identify a worthy emotion, then twist it to an evil end. One illustration will suffice, which I am sure you will have no difficulty in relating to more recent events.

Towards the end of the eighth century, Scorrier noted two factors; the desire to bring peace to England, which had suffered war ever since the Romans left, and the power of a group of flint-knappers operating in Grime's Graves in Suffolk (where they had been operating happily in the same way for over 1,000 years). The King of Anglia, Ethelgruba, was hanging on by his toenails, and needed all the support he could get. Scorrier pointed out to the flint-knappers that if they made their support conditional on a substantial subsidy for flints, they could hold Ethelgruba to ransom. Under Scorrier's guidance, they did this. Beginning by applying the tax revenues of his kingdom, Ethelgruba realized that there was scope for spreading the burden. He approached his colleague Ethelwasta of Wessex, whose hold on the throne depended on continuing to subsidize a recalcitrant cell of flax-scutchers in Piddletrenthide.

The two agreed that their interests coincided. They jointly approached their brethren Ethelwapa of Mercia, Etheltura of Northumbria and Ruthless the Great, Emperor of Rutland, with the suggestion that universal peace would benefit them all. Their intention to apply the tax revenues of the whole of England to the flint-knappers and flax-scutchers was not, at this stage, revealed.

USE

The plan worked perfectly. By the end of the ninth century, the flint-knappers continued to enjoy a subsidy for every flint knapped, and had filled Grime's Graves with a 'mountain' of unwanted flints. The peat workings in Norfolk known as the 'Broads' were being used for additional storage, to the disgust of the locals, who depended for their living on hiring coracles to tourists. (This was called a 'flint lake'.) The 'mountains' of unused scutched flax from Piddletrenthide were being carted as far afield as the headwaters of the river Exe, where they so affected the drainage that a large area of hitherto fertile farmland became a useless moor. Schemes for exporting flints to the Picts, who desperately needed them for building brochs, and flax to the Welsh, whose traditional use of woad caused widespread hypothermia, had not been pursued for complex economic and political reasons.

The sovereign kingdoms of Anglia, Wessex, Mercia, Northumbria and the Empire of Rutland had, to the universal displeasure of their inhabitants, been formed into a federal union then known as The United States of England. A common currency had been introduced, based on the groat.

A number of bloody rebellions by the coracle owners and Exmoor farmers had to be crushed, causing damage to several of the king's hunting forests and rabbit warrens. For a while, the situation showed signs of getting out of hand, but Scorrier's ingenuity was equal to the occasion. He daringly suggested continuing payment for producing nothing at all; the knappers should be paid for every pit and the scutchers for every floor they took out of production, or 'set-aside' as he called it. There were many within the Council of ICM who felt this preposterous suggestion was going too far, but Scorrier's judgement was vindicated. Faced with the danger that, if subsidies were reduced, the kings would lose their thrones and their bureaucrats might even have to be redeployed, his proposal was accepted. The flint-knappers grew rich for doing nothing, and turned Grime's Graves into a tourist attraction. The flax-scutchers went abroad, renting their cottages to merchants from London. The rest of England grew steadily poorer under the weight of taxes, and would undoubtedly have rebelled successfully had an invasion from Normandy not saved that day.

As you will know, Scorrier has recently applied this technique more broadly within western Europe. However, for some time now he has been seeking more creative outlets and, whilst final decisions have not yet been taken, I can reveal some of his current thinking.

One of the most obvious areas of over-production at the present time is in education. Under the influence of the education lobby, the number of graduates has spiralled out of control, to a point where there is no possibility of their being used. However, abandoning the present system of financing educational institutions would obviously risk industrial action by professors, vice chancellors, telephonists and other key personnel which makes it politically unthinkable. Schemes have been proposed for stockpiling MBAs, or supplying them at nominal price to Third World or ex-communist countries, but these also are considered impracticable. Scorrier's simple but brilliant solution is Academic Set-aside. Under this arrangement, universities opting for the set-aside grant will be mothballed. All staff will continue to be paid full salary, on the strict understanding they do no work whatever. (The difference will in many cases be difficult to detect, but a new Academic Inspectorate is being formed, as a branch of the enlarged Health and Safety Executive, to undertake the task.) The buildings will be left open as nature reserves or squats for unemployed business studies graduates.

Other proposed schemes, such as subsidizing Japanese car manufacturers to stockpile cars in Mount Fujiyama, and paying set-aside to pop groups, are less likely to be approved.

Grants are a more hopeful area in which to snare Buckden. The best-known form of grant is payable on the basis of *where* something is done. An area, or even a country, is designated as in need of special support, and thereafter given anything it wants, and many things it does not. The only beneficiaries of the grant are, of course, the firms doing the work and the bureaucrats paying the money.

Grants may also be tied to specific projects. Tempters who have been in the field for a while are prone, at this point, to mutter 'groundnuts to you'. By doing so, they are showing their age; for several decades now, the fall-back project has been dams. We have, in fact, produced clear rules for the objective and unbiased guidance of bureaucrats and politicians when selecting projects. Projects should be:

- large
- visible
- prestigious
- supportive of the arms industry
- pleasing to local politicians
- likely to generate votes
- capable of supporting large numbers of bureaucrats

Value to inhabitants of the areas concerned is, of course, irrelevant.

For Buckden to make progress in this area will not be easy. Garden gnomes have not so far been seen as having defence implications, or adding to the prestige of heads of state or local councillors. There is, however, one particularly ingenious form of grant which is of almost limitless application and may be helpful in his destruction. This is a brainchild of my own, and I call it the *Homing Grant*. The grant is designed to give two weak governments mutual support. It works as follows.

Let us suppose that the British and Ruritanian governments are both in a weak position with their electorates.

After discussion, a supposed need is identified in one country (we will suppose this to be Ruritania, but it could equally well be Britain). It is of no consequence what the 'need' is, provided it is acceptable to the politicians of both areas. Let us imagine, for example, that a 'need' has been agreed between both governments for fish and chip shops to be established in Ruritania. An arrangement is then made to set up a British Advisory Fund for the Establishment of Fish and Chip Shops in Ruritania (BAFEFCSR – an unintelligible acronym is often a distinct advantage).

From this, everyone will feel they have benefited. The Ruritanian government will be able to claim that they are active in the interests of their people. The international standing and influence of the country has been demonstrated by the provision of the Fund. The population of Ruritania, which has so far managed without fish and chip shops, will gain from additional employment and improved nutrition. They will also feel part of the civilized world, which has long enjoyed this delicacy.

The British government will claim that they are fulfilling their moral obligations to the developing and needy parts of the world. They will please the supporters of free enterprise and high principles. The administration of the Fund will require a new Agency staffed by civil servants; for them, there will be frequent trips to Ruritania. The Union of Fish and Chip Executives will be delighted, as will the fishing industry, the manufacturers of frozen chips, the makers of fish friers and the collectors of old newspapers.

But more than anyone, British Consultants will be laughing all the way to the bank. Theirs will be the job of providing advice and consultancy in the establishment of the new industry, and training its operatives. It is to them that the money in the British Advisory Fund for the Establishment of Fish and Chip Shops in Ruritania will be paid. You will now appreciate why I have called this the Homing Fund.

The Homing Fund principle can also be adapted to purely national use; in this case it is called an *Initiative*. Initiatives are a device by which bureaucrats, politicians and an organized vested interest identify a 'need' to satisfy for which 'resources can be made available'. In making the choice, the guiding principle is that as few vested interests as possible should feel they are damaged by the choice, or at least that those that do are weak and inarticulate. Let us suppose (for example) that the parties agree that a suitable 'need' exists for the encouragement of tatting as a cottage industry. The appropriate government department will then make a series of grants available for tatters, set up an internal Tatting Directorate, fund research on tatting either by consultants or within the universities, engage PR consultants, set up regional Tatting Offices, and hold a media launch at a conference centre in Westminster addressed by the President of the Department Himself. I do not need to explain exactly who the beneficiaries of such an initiative would be.

You should be aware that we have ourselves used this source of funds for, of course, entirely valid reasons. Naturally, the ICM regularly avails itself of whatever grants fall within its field of competence. It has indeed been signally successful. We have been awarded a number of grants by Training and Enterprise Councils. Following the personal commitment of the All Lowest to the development of His staff, The Huntingdonshire TEC accepted our application for a grant towards accreditation as an Investor in People (IIP). The grant was small, but will prove a useful addition to the Chief Tempter's Benevolent Fund.

(Perhaps I should say here that, following a visit by a well-known firm of management consultants, His Lowness has also been convinced that the standing of the Lowerarchy will also be enhanced by obtaining accreditation under both BS5750 and ISO9000 quality standards.

Without this, we shall also be excluded from most work within local and central government. However, as some of our procedures are slightly unusual, there has been difficulty in finding suitable assessors.)

Other grants have been awarded to ICM under the Know-How Fund (establishing blast furnaces in Siberia), Phare (training fire-fighters in the Bosphorus), and Tacis (research in vulcanology in the Urals). We also have been successful in obtaining a large contract for the training of EU Commission staff in methods for the destruction of surplus food supplies.

The ICM itself also offers a limited number of grants for suitable research and training activities. I may say here that most of the stories about the way these grants were distributed are completely without foundation - or at least without any definite proof. It is true that the Tormentors' Extra-curricular Extension Directorate (TEED) infiltrated the Management School of the University of Pinner. The entire cleaning staff of the School and all nineteen professors were turned, following receipt of information about photography sessions held in the first year language laboratory. It is *not* true that the £1m grant to the School was made on the condition that a set of all prints were made available to every TEED director; only selected prints were distributed.

Likewise, it *is* true that research grants of £500,000 each were made available to thirteen consultancy organizations, all based on a semi-detached house in Ponders End. There were, however, valid reasons for this. The fact that each happened to be headed by the mistress of a TEED director, guaranteed their bona fides. That it was the same director (and mistress) in each case was a further proof of the integrity of the organizations. It is admitted that applications for these grants were in some cases subject to a little delay. The carping criticism levelled by one applicant who had to wait rather more than eighteen months was, however, ungracious in the extreme, as each application had, for obvious reasons, to be thoroughly scrutinized by a team of expert assessors.

You should consider carefully whether this formula could be adapted to Buckden's business; whilst the need for gnome-making technology in the economy of the developing countries is not immediately obvious, I feel sure that a creative approach would find some opening. You may suggest to Sir Andrew that his lack of market penetration in Eastern Europe could be compensated by a new gnome plant in the Ukraine. The Watchers tell us that he has never applied to the EU for funding. There could be enormous scope here for tying up his resources.

The Good cause is perhaps the purest example of the application of Buttercrambe's definition to politicking in business. The method is simplicity itself. Some action, product or legislation that might be thought of as in the general interest is identified. The only criterion is that whatever is chosen must appear credible at the time; the more credible, the greater the leverage. Over the years, we have used an immense range of factors – some real, many imagined. A particularly neat example is the phrase 'Roads, hospitals and schools', universally employed by politicians to sum up the benefits to be purchased by any form of additional taxation; the roads lobby chuckle with glee every time it is used. Health and safety is a productive area; the tyre and car windscreen industries have blessed us for that, although cycling helmets are so far proving rather more difficult.

There may be an opportunity here for exploitation of the ICC rivalry. As Sir Andrew, Buckden will find many doors opened to him that were hitherto closed. I think you could put it into his mind to lobby some vulnerable member of the government to introduce draconian new legislation which will have the effect of driving most garden centres, including ICC, out of business. Something to do with plant disease should do the trick. Perhaps a new Inspectorate of Plant Health, financed by a levy on the industry could be established. I would dearly like to suggest the foundation of a pressure group for Vegetable Rights, but I fear that the time for that is not yet quite with us.

The use of **Taxes** to enhance competitive advantage is a specialized activity, and not generally recommended. Its successful applications are comparatively rare. One of the most spectacular was the lobbying campaign by late eighteenth-century stonemasons and brickies which resulted in the introduction of the Window Tax. Attempts by the chewing gum lobby to drive smokers into their arms through ever higher tobacco taxes have had little success. I cannot at the moment picture a tax which would help Buckden in his fight against ICC, but any attempt by the makers of sundials to have a Gnome Tax introduced should be encouraged.

I must now direct your attention to the second main subdivision of this Sin; **internal politicking**, or politicking with a small 'p'.

Internal politicking begins with picking the right subordinates; those whom the manager can bully and manipulate. Recruitment is a specialized area. Thanks to the work of the Headhunting division of the ICM, a code has been established which not only hides managers' political intentions from other humans, but also allows them to deceive each other. Let us suppose there is a vacancy for a senior manager in their organization. In order to recruit, they will (unless nepotism is used) draw up some kind of a specification of the person they are seeking, which will then be translated into an advertisement or a brief for a headhunter. Irrespective of the nature of the job, the specification will usually run something like this:

The person we require will be dynamic, creative, an

> excellent communicator, motivated and above all a good team player, able to lead an established team of young self-starters. You will be able to demonstrate the highest level of achievement, and will be used to working at board level. A superb package is offered for the right individual.

Every word of this is, of course, coded nonsense. If such an individual was recruited, he or she would be out on their ear within a week and their colleagues would have resigned or been carried to the nearest asylum still in business. The real requirement is as follows:

> Must be able to demonstrate that he is one of us. Arrogant and self-opinionated, but with the political skills to know when and how to keep quiet, when to talk and shoot his mouth off, how to stab colleagues in the back, when to creep and when to show off. Insatiably greedy. Well-versed in the latest jargon and buzz-words. Aware that the only true crime is to get caught. Unable to show us up or make us feel uncomfortable; either incompetent or capable of appearing at least as incompetent as the rest of us.

There are more similarities between ordinary, low-level office politics and politics at board level than you may realize. The basic skills remain the same. Like his more junior colleagues, the CE must be able to maintain level eye contact and a warm, friendly voice while lying through his teeth. He must be able to shake the hand of someone whose reputation and career he is planning to destroy with warmth and camaraderie. He must know the Eight Ways of Implying Total Agreement without committing himself to anything. He must be practised in the Thirteen Methods for Responding to Direct Questions Without Giving a Quotable Answer. He must be able to distinguish winners from losers before others do, and know how to ingratiate himself with the former as certainly as he distances himself from the latter. He must know the techniques for weakening others' positions in private while supporting them in public. He must be able to judge the moment to plunge the knife in a colleague's back, and the sort of smile to wear whilst doing so. He must be adept in kicking someone who is already down whilst appearing to help them on to their feet. He must know when to desert a sinking ship.

All these competences are as important in the Boardroom as in the Open Plan Office, but a CE must be taught to play on a much bigger field. There are also certain weapons open to CEs that have little power at lower levels. If, when he was a junior manager, Buckden had threatened to resign unless he got his way he would have been handed his P45 within the hour. If he had ganged up openly with a number of his colleagues and tried to obtain the dismissal of a group of his opponents he would have been not only disciplined but possibly sued. If he had made an open bid to take over the work of another division, factory or whatever, he would have been laughed out of his job.

As a director, all this has changed. Because they have reserved their places on the Golden Gravy Train, CEs' politicking need not necessarily be in secret. As members of the same Club, they know that much of what they do is shadow-boxing. They may succeed in engineering the resignation of a colleague, but they will know that within the month he will be re-employed, probably at a higher salary, and certainly with a substantial golden handshake. If they win a hostile takeover bid for a rival, they can rest assured that the only people to suffer from the subsequent reorganization will be the junior staff for whom redundancy will mean at best grave domestic disorganization, and at worst penury and a ruined career. For Buckden and his fellow passengers on the Gravy Train it will mean a shot of adrenalin, a raised profile and an increase of capital.

This then, is the next field in which you must joist with your newly-dubbed Knight. It is a large one in which he may get lost. It is littered with ingenious traps, and there are monsters of all kinds waiting for him round every corner. The growing confidence I have in you tells me that you will enjoy ruining Sir Andrew's attempts at directorial politicking. In particular, do not forget my suggestion about the Inspectorate of Plant Health, and let him keep his eye firmly on Smithers' progress in the Honours Stakes. I shall enjoy my holiday in the dungeons awaiting your next report.

Your loving Uncle

Barripper

Instrument 3: POLITICKING

INSTRUCTIONS

Simply agree or disagree with the following statements. The outcomes are insignificant, although the results may change your life permanently.

1. Caution and reserve are the key to success.
2. There may be trouble ahead.
3. When you enter the room you are barely noticed.
4. Losing your rhythm can throw you off balance.
5. Your preferred manner of relaxing is reading the newspapers.
6. In discussion, jump in, strike low and step back.
7. The growth of the split infinitive is to be widely lamented.
8. Bringing home the bacon can land you in the soup.
9. Pretence is princely but dissimulation is regal.
10. Chasing red herrings is necessary for the opportunist.
11. The world will be a different place in the next century.
12. Castles in the air are a source of mystery.

13. The UK's position in Europe causes untold problems.

14. Macramé and origami make strange bedfellows.

15. The *Titanic* was doomed from the start.

SCORING

1. Be wary of this one. It could be that you are just not sharp enough to spot opportunities.
   Agree 7 Disagree 4

2. There will always be trouble ahead but anticipation can create openings.
   Agree 4 Disagree 8

3. On balance an asset unless you are totally lacking in personality.
   Agree 7 Disagree 3

4. Yes but the true opportunist will quickly swing to a new rhythm.
   Agree 2 Disagree 8

5. The origin of all lies and deceit.
   Agree 10 Disagree 0

6. Strike low yes, step back yes, but never, never jump in.
   Agree 2 Disagree 6

7. A useful put-down, but not to be overdone.
   Agree 5 Disagree 2

8. Yes, but buttering someone up could be throwing money down the drain.
   Score 5 whatever.

9. No question.
   Agree 12 Disagree 0

10. No, it's for someone else.
    Agree 0 Disagree 10

11. All a question of perspective; it's not so very far away.
    Score 5 whatever.

12. Not to the artful. He knows how to keep them suspended.
    Agree 1 Disagree 9

13. And great opportunities for those with friends in Brussels.
    Agree 2 Disagree 8

14. No. Going to bed with someone whomsoever necessary is the first rule of the politician.
    Agree 0 Disagree 10

15. Not necessarily. It was always worth a shot.
    Agree 3 Disagree 7.

ANALYSIS

Below 50: on occasions you fancy yourself as a politician, but . . . really, you are a no-hoper. Abandon flighty dreams, buckle down and concentrate on an honest day's work.

51–89: although your political acumen shows promise, you may well find that promise is the only outcome. You have some truly great skills but fail too often to make the final twist of the knife.

90+: what is holding you back? A role in politics is wasted when a fortune in kick-backs is yours for the taking. Do not share your gift with others; it is born, not made.

Chapter 4
Clubbability

'He marks – not that you won or lost –
But how you played the game.'
GRANTLAND RICE

My dear Relubbus

What a pity that your attempt to set up an Inspectorate of Plant Health failed. It was a noble effort on your part, and you should not be discouraged. Your error was in your choice of a contact for Sir Andrew to lobby on the subject. To select a junior minister in the Department of Trade and Industry whose only weakness was a secret passion for model railways was naïve in the extreme.

Such childish occupations rarely form fertile ground for character assassination, however much they may be laughed at. Certainly as a Trainee Tempter I did succeed in destroying a manager who was addicted to collecting cigarette cards, and the story is instructive. He began harmlessly enough, merely spending time that should have been devoted to budget preparation in telling his secretary about the latest additions to his collection. However, I was alert to the possibilities of the situation. One evening when his wife happened to be visiting her parents, I inspired him to invite his secretary to view what he had. Needless to say, his wife came home early. After one of the most colourful arguments I have ever witnessed, she threw his collection into a wheely-bin. More importantly, she reported the matter to his director the next morning, and he was instantly dismissed for sexual harassment and breach of company policy on relationships. The last I heard of him, he was selling candy floss with a touring circus. Perhaps the most amusing aspect of the episode is that he never actually touched the girl; cigarette cards were of considerably more interest to him than sex.

However, few women display serious interest in model railways. Given time, you might have found a way forward by making the obsession widely known amongst the more cynical of the minister's fellow MPs or senior civil servants in his department. You might also have tried introducing him to some of the more expensive collector's items. Even his resources might have felt the strain if he had been persuaded to purchase pre-war boxed sets of Hornby Double-O in mint condition.

The simple fact is that knowledge of this hobby did not offer Sir Andrew a sufficient hold to persuade him to lobby his colleagues to set up a brand new Inspectorate. This battle in his war against ICC has therefore been lost. I also sense a danger that you yourself may start playing with these trivial knickknacks when you should be about the business of Tempting. This would, of course, be a serious offence.

However, you can now move on to tempt Buckden with the fourth sin: *The sin of Clubbability*. This is a recent addition to the canon, and there are some experienced Tempters who have not yet grasped its significance. It is, however, one of the most exciting developments I have led for the last ten aeons, and encapsulates some of the best work by the lads in the Management Destruction Unit (MDU). I will try to explain first what it is, then why it is so useful to us, and finally explain the ways in which Buckden is already guilty of it.

Clubbability is the predilection to belong to organizations which are neither family nor business in nature. The purposes of clubs are as many as there are human interests.

Most clubs are in themselves harmless, and the act of belonging to a club may also be harmless. However, both clubs and membership of clubs have led many into our arms, and you must understand how this happens and how *you* can make it happen.

We must begin by considering the nature of clubs themselves; many, as I have said, are apparently innocent in intention. Morris dancing, glee clubs, family history societies and the like are rarely hotbeds of iniquity. Indeed, some of the most doubtful-sounding clubs are often the most moral; members of all-in wrestling and fencing clubs are renowned for their clean, healthy life-styles.

However, by the same token, amateur dramatic societies, bridge and tennis clubs and other jolly, social activities can, when carried out in clubs, become the source of every kind of evil. Members of these organizations use them to compensate for their failure in the real business of life, and, under our guidance, display the grossest egotism, backbiting and enjoyment in slandering their enemies and any not of their coterie. Such organizations frequently prove to be sinks of unbelievable iniquity. It is often possible to arrange for members to accuse each other of cheating, for example. Once made, such charges are usually sufficient to ensure the total ruination of both parties; our Legal Aid Directorate will ensure the diversion of their assets to our hard-working and loyal agents in what is still called the 'legal profession'. There is a window of opportunity here. Buckden is a member of the Croynge golf club; the Watchers tell me that Smithers is a member too. Ensure Buckden becomes aware of Smithers' membership, and bring them together in the rough, or at the nineteenth hole, as soon as possible.

Clubs based on shared background – old boys' and old girls' clubs, sororities, fraternities, alumni clubs, associations – even annual reunions of groups that have lived together – can have a surprisingly powerful effect on their members. The loyalty to such groups may, if stirred up carefully, become feverish. It can outweigh ties to partner, family, employer or community. Buckden is a regular attender at the Old Walloponians' annual dinner; look back on the trouble he got into last November between the hors d'oeuvres and the Loyal Toast when his speech resulted in raising three rousing choruses of independence for Walloponia. Incitement to revolt brought him close to the clutches of the police. His escape, and its concealment from the Press are still marks of what you are up against.

Many organizations, including one or two to which Buckden belongs, are not called clubs, but have the characteristics of clubs. He is, for example, the President of United's Senior Dining Room. This is similar to the 'messes' (or 'wardrooms') which are central to the life of officers in units of the armed services – regiments, corps, ships, stations. These organizations have proved of immense value to us, and it is essential that you understand their working.

There is an ill-defined borderline between clubs and what can, depending on the membership, be called unions, guilds, associations or institutions. The role of such bodies in preserving the supposed interests of their members at the expense of all outside is well known. It is this which makes the Club such a powerful weapon in Buckden's destruction.

The most evil (and therefore more useful) are clubs which have either no declared purpose, or declare a purpose which is clearly no more than a front. The former are typified by the 'gentlemen's clubs' in London. The wickedness that brews behind the portals of Boodle's or the Reform is unimaginable to most. Naturally the All Lowest is a member at the Athenaeum and I myself belong to White's. Clubs that have a declared aim which hides their true purpose are probably the most maleficent of all. Few members of the Marylebone Cricket Club (MCC), for example, have ever played cricket in Marylebone. The garish colours of the club – vivid stripes of yellow and bright red – appear to some as a yet unidentified link with our own operations. The true purpose of this extraordinary organization is still due to be investigated by some of our best agents. Unfortunately none has yet come up for election.

Although their real agenda remains a source of mystery, members appear to understand an unwritten code to which they blindly adhere. Secrecy is again the key. Breaking the code is tantamount to being 'found out', or even worse, 'made public'. The true brotherhood of the Club is never more apparent than when it is required to judge an application for membership. Many employ 'blackballing' – a procedure whereby one or two existing members can prevent acceptance of an applicant for reasons of their own, despite the wishes of the majority.

You have told me that Buckden is hoping to be invited to speak at the Annual Dinner of the Livery Company – the Worshipful Company of Dustmen and Sewage Artisans – of which he is a member. This is excellent news.

You may not know the history of the Livery Company of the Worshipful Company of Dustmen and Sewage Artisans. This was a late mediaeval trade union, notable for restrictive practices designed to ensure its members life-long employment and enforced on pain of death by drowning in a cesspit. The Company regarded the Black Death (in the fifteenth century) and the Great Plague of London (1665) as its greatest achievements, both resulting from prolonged strikes by its members. The eighteenth and early nineteenth centuries, however, were periods in which industrial action proved unnecessary. A combination of extortionate subscriptions and fortunate investment decisions resulted in an accumulation of wealth by what had become a moribund organization. At this stage, the remains of the Company were taken over by a group of wealthy Victorian businessmen, who turned it into a benevolent association, mutual admiration society and dining club.

You would feel at home in the Company. Membership is limited to one hundred. When a vacancy occurs, replacements must be proposed and seconded by existing Members of at least thirty years' standing from amongst

> Godfearing Christians who have demonstrated their commitment to the ancient and honourable mystery of the removal of debris, dirt, dregs, dross, garbage, offal, ordure, refuse and scrap, are able to show assets of not less than £1m, and were either educated at a recognized public school or commissioned in a decent regiment.

Naturally there are no female Members.

The Company is based in a 'Hall' in the graveyard of a derelict church in the City of London, which was built in 1888 to a Gothic design originally intended for a waiting room at Shoeburyness Station. It is sumptuously furnished, with genuine oil portraits of the Worshipful Masters on the walls. Naturally the food is both bad and prohibitively expensive. The cellar of the Company is renowned, and is commonly thought to contain sufficient wine to drown the entire membership. The Members' livery consists of Jacobean Dustmen's uniform done in velvet with ermine facings. It is worn only twice a year. On the first occasion, those members capable of doing so process in the Lord Mayor's Show, carrying silver slop buckets and ordure scrapers. The second is the Installation of the Worshipful Master, which takes place in the Hall on the anniversary of the start of the Great Fire of London. On presenting himself, each Member deposits a symbolic bunnybag of kitchen refuse in a wheely-bin at the door. The in-coming Master enters to the strains of 'My Old

Man's a Dustman' played by a string quartet in the minstrels' gallery. Fifteen toasts are proposed and answered, and Members' chauffeurs collect their charges between one and two in the morning.

All this may seem harmless play-acting. Indeed, there are some similar organizations that try to frustrate our work through support of 'good causes'. We have singled these out, and their eventual doom is assured. However, the Worshipful Company of Dustmen and Sewage Artisans is not one of these. Its main function is mutual back-slapping and preferment. Through it, Buckden regularly meets those who will help him, with ever-increasing speed and certainty, into our clutches.

The other kind of club is the secret society. These are one of the few ways in which we have chosen to interfere openly and directly in human affairs, and as such you will have learnt the basics at ICM. As the continued anonymity of these organizations is crucial to their value to us, it is permissible only to refer to them by their codenames

(Society A and Society B) whatever the level of clearance of those communicating. You will have been given the necessary information during your final briefing by IRRE. They are key elements in our strategies to destroy mankind. Both operate at many levels, but both are particularly relevant to management destruction.

Society A was the brainchild of Goyte. Its conception is a remarkable story. One rainy afternoon in the mid-eighteenth century Goyte was confined, for reasons which need not concern us, in the potting shed of a minister of the Scottish church. In search of a means of passing the time, Goyte fell to looking over the various articles in the shed – tools, a tattered copy of the Old Testament, a pair of the minister's gardening trousers, and numerous other odd and unrelated leavings. He had been trained in memory-enhancing techniques based on association, and rapidly memorized everything within sight. It so happened that he was also an expert in guilt-raising by dream techniques, and it occurred to him that he could wreak havoc with the minister's already minimal sanity by instructing him, in a dream, that the future of the human race depended on the regular verbatim recital by a priestly élite of a meaningless list of these items.

The minister was even then enjoying his usual post-prandial nap, and Goyte duly appeared to him wearing some workman's clothing he had found in the shed. To his main message, he added a series of amusing threats as to what would happen to the minister or his priests if the list was ever misquoted or its contents divulged to outsiders. The minister, who had been under Goyte's care for some time, and was already almost in our clutches, obeyed the instructions to the letter, and rapidly gathered a group of initiates about him.

The strength and growth of what had begun as a childish game filling an hour of enforced idleness amazed even Goyte, but he quickly saw its value. Starting within the

Celtic fringes of the United Kingdom, Society A has spread almost worldwide, although its greatest strength remains in western Europe. This stroke of genius was duly rewarded when Goyte was lowered to the dignity of Arch-tempter.

You will hear a number of contradictory misrepresentations of the significance of Society A, both from those inside and those without. Even most of those within it have only a dim and partial understanding of its structure and operation. Some would have us believe that it remains a childish game suitable for whiling away a rainy afternoon and is of no practical importance. Others claim that it is a movement inspired by and dedicated to the service of our Eternal Enemy. Some even believe it is part of our operation. Few have grasped its real significance.

Buckden is not a member of Society A, but is aware that many of those with whom he deals are. Thanks to Goyte's inspired work, nearly a third of those with whom he does business have succumbed to this childishness. This is an increasing cause of anxiety to him, and his doubts as to the effects of this and the way he should handle it have damaged his judgement on several occasions. He has considered whether he should join, despite regarding the Society with contempt. Tempt him to do so; he will despise himself for his hypocrisy, and may suffer the ignominy of failing.

Society B is even more widespread, and is almost the only human organization openly and generally understood to be devoted to our cause. It also began in western Europe, although a good deal further south than Society A. In setting it up, we decided (unlike Society A) not to disguise its true purpose or to trick it out with meaningless toys and trivia. The residents of the area in which we established it wanted only a means of furthering their own ends and those of their families, at the expense of their neighbours. This we rapidly furnished to them. The results have been a perpetual delight; blackmail, murder, torture, extortion, drug addiction, and almost every other form of depravity. Society B has also spread worldwide; where it has not reached, it has been copied.

Before you become too enthusiastic about Society B, I must point out its limitations in the work you have in hand. Sadly Buckden and his kind have so far proved resistant to its attractions, and many perceive that it is our invention. You may feel this betokens a meanness of spirit, cowardice and lack of proper self-interest; if so, I agree with you. However, these attitudes have so far defied our best efforts to break them down; I do not recommend that you waste a moment's thought in attempting to persuade Buckden to throw in his lot with Society B.

The second aspect of clubs, and in many ways the more important to our work, is the attitude they engender in their members, irrespective of their declared aims. At its most powerful, the club controls much of the behaviour of those involved. Those affected will think, before any major decision, not about what is best, but about what is expected by their fellow members.

Many of the most powerful of clubs have no actual existence. They operate by an unspoken understanding of common interest, often between individuals in different – even conflicting roles. Thus politicians of all parties belong, in fact, to the same club, as do all the hangers-on of politics: political commentators, media interviewers and correspondents. After a convivial drink or meal together, they will adopt poses of disagreement and dispute for the benefit of those outside their club – ie the general public – and then go back arm-in-arm for a nightcap. Writers and critics will swap roles, reviewing each other's work and praising each other's achievements. Our agents the barristers will engage in the mock battles of the courtroom before returning to their robing room in the happy unity of an exclusive and luxurious club wholly supported by outside subscriptions. Medical practitioners will close ranks against any of their customers who dare to enquire about the goings-on inside. CEs such as Buckden, who are theoretically at each other's throats, belong to the managers' club and will stand together as an army against any in the outside world who might threaten them.

All clubs have their methods by which members recognize each other. These include.

- handshakes
- ties
- badges
- accents and modes of speech
- name-dropping

For members of Secret Society A, recognition is by handshake. The same is true of the Boy Scout movement. The difference is fairly easy for those of average intelligence to distinguish when sober, but Goyte arranged for a Production Director who was also District Scout Commissioner to confuse them. The victim's reaction when, later that day, he was invited into a circle of elderly men in fancy dress and ordered to roll up his trouser leg on pain of death by torture was a joy to behold. Goyte has tried the opposite confusion on several of his charges, but never actually managed, as he put it, to 'Tie them into knots'. Goyte has a particularly juvenile sense of humour.

Many clubs still use the time-worn recognition device of a necktie. This has the advantage of automatically excluding those who do not wear ties, such as men of non-Anglo-Saxon origin, inferior social status, and women. It is relatively unimportant what institution the tie represents; it doesn't even matter whether the wearer went to it; wearing one of these ties indicates adherence to the system. The sartorial design unit of ICM has come up with some quite remarkable ensembles over the years, several of which give me a chuckle every time I stumble upon them.

The use of badges to indicate club membership, is confined to loco spotters, twitchers, religious fundamentalists and members of darts teams. You will not find Buckden wearing one. Do not make the attempt.

Recognition of the most powerful clubs is achieved by accent and mode of speech. Some decades ago a double agent named Mitford published an extensive listing of the means by which upper-class English identified their fellow club members (the 'U speakers') from the rest of the world (the 'non-U'). You must learn how the same technique is used by members of Buckden's Chief Executives' Club to classify those they meet as either one of them (a 'C speaker') or one of the rest (the 'non-C'). Non-Cs are also immediately recognizable by a number of distinguishing characteristics such as brown shoes, beards, five-o'clock shadow, speaking German, button-down collars and suits from Burton the Tailor. You will learn to be a little more perceptive in discerning state-school background, a lower-second class honours degree and a local dialect.

It is however principally by the use of words that Cs and non-Cs can be identified. The full manual is available from the ICM Publications Department; here are a few extracts to give you its flavour.

C speaker	*Non-C speaker*
I'll get my people to sort that out	I'm afraid that is too complicated for me to understand
We must all sing from the same hymnsheet	We had better tell the same lies
He came off the wall at us	He had no idea what he was talking about
Let's interface on that later	We'll have a meeting tomorrow

Could you run that past me again?	Sorry, I was thinking about my golf swing
I'll get my PA to call you	I haven't a clue what you're on about

Name-dropping is a key method of recognition for most clubs. You must learn to recognize the right and wrong ways to use this powerful technique. It is best to approach this by an iterative technique, rather like the card game of 'Cheat'. Each player, as you will remember, throws a card face down and declares its value, which must be higher than that of the previous player. The next player must either accept what is claimed and throw a yet higher card, or challenge what the previous player has said. If two CEs met for the first time at a conference, the technique might work like this:

A (casually): 'I was with Bloggs yesterday and he told me interest rates are going down in a matter of days.'
B (even more casually): 'That's interesting. Snodgrass and I were at the IMF in Toronto only last week and he was saying the next move would certainly be upwards.'
A (with slight emphasis): 'I'm not sure that would be the view of old Porterhouse. When I was down at his place the other day he assured me that monetarism had had its day.'
B (ingenuously): 'Porterhouse?'
A (patronizingly): 'Lord Porterhouse. Chairman of the International Banking Union until last year.'
B (even more ingenuously): 'I thought he was dead.'

A is likely, at this point, to recognize an old friend at the opposite side of the room.

Expert name-dropping naturally calls for correct choice of name. There is little to be gained by dropping names that will not be recognized, or of those under investigation by the Serious Fraud Office or the Vice Squad. It also requires a good level of verbal competence. Suitable phrases include:

> 'Brown is always pulling my leg about our trip to the EU Ministerial Conference in Geneva.'
> 'Jones was asking what I thought of his latest interview on *Newsnight*.'
> 'Smith was one of the most brilliant in my time at Oxford.'

Playing cheat and name-dropping culminate in the Bluffers' Club. This again has no written rules or stated membership criteria, but the Bluffer will be found in every club in the land. The ease with which abuse of position, shallow knowledge and a sharp tongue can extinguish honest inquiry and worthwhile debate grows with practice and feeds off self-promotion. Remember that it is not sufficient merely to appear to be knowledgeable, it is to do it with aggravating nonchalance. The Bluffer is above correction and rebuke; he exists in a time-warp of total self-belief.

You may ask how all this will help to destroy Buckden. The point is that he is not a member of the 'right' clubs, and is deeply worried by this fact. The definition of 'temptation' which you will have learnt by heart on the morning of your first day at ICM is:

> Exploiting a virtuous urge to beget vicious behaviour.

The stronger the urge, the more vicious the behaviour.

Buckden's urge to be recognized as a member of the best clubs offers immense scope; now he has his K, your task is much easier. With good tradecraft you will be able to make him seem foolish in the eyes of those he wishes to impress, squander money he cannot afford, dissipate time needed for the running of his business, alienate his wife and family, fall into the clutches of those who will do him harm, and roll up his trouser leg at an inopportune moment.

I look forward to your next report. Go to it!

Your loving Uncle

Barripper

PS Do not forget the Croynge golf club.

Instrument 4: CLUBBABILITY

INSTRUCTIONS

In each section, tick the word that describes you most accurately, even if it sounds completely unlike you. If you don't understand a word, make a wild guess.

1 a) Dozy
b) Sensuous
c) Curious

2 a) Excitable
b) Nonchalant
c) Ineffectual

3 a) Antipathetic
b) Disturbed
c) Passionate

4 a) Obsessive
b) Disorganized
c) Moronic

5 a) Frustrated
b) Platonic
c) Fulfilled

6 a) Overweening
b) Depraved
c) Bumptious

7 a) Interactive
b) Lapidary
c) Lazy

8 a) Querulous
b) Lackadaisical
c) Bucolic

9 a) Laconic
b) Frumpish
c) Jolly

SCORING

1. a 1 b 0 c 2
2. a 0 b 2 c 1
3. a 2 b 1 c 0
4. a 0 b 1 c 2
5. a 1 b 0 c 2
6. a 1 b 0 c 2
7. a 2 b 0 c 1
8. a 0 b 1 c 2
9. a 1 b 0 c 2

ANALYSIS

18–14: you are obsessively clubbable, and can be persuaded to join anything and everything.

13–9: you are likely to waste time and money on one or two assorted clubs.

8–4: you are not all that interested in clubs, and should be tempted in some other way.

3–0: you should become a hermit.

Chapter 5
Greed

'He has not acquired a fortune, the fortune has acquired him.'

BION

My dear Relubbus

The idea of persuading Buckden to apply for membership of the Beefsteak Club was excellent. The fact that there is a division of the United Group promoting vegan food had obviously escaped his mind. What a pity news of his blackballing just happened to be released to the Press! Well done, but much more will be needed before he is destroyed.

The fifth Sin is *The Sin of Greed*. The lust for more – more money, more food, more fame, more possessions, more power – is the main engine of the destruction of the human world as we have now made it. The increasing anger Sir Andrew feels about the effect of United's competitor, ICC, is rapidly destroying him. We already know how it has wounded his pride; now it is wounding his pocket. The Watchers have drawn my attention to the fact that, because of this competition, United's sales have fallen rapidly within the last two years. This has naturally started to affect their profitability which, in turn, has affected Sir Andrew's bonus. This has fallen from £1.2m last year to under £500,000 this. You should have discovered this and reported it to me. With such motivation, the chance of self-destructive action on his part is immeasurably increased.

To satisfy their greed, some people adopt a life of overt criminality, becoming burglars, muggers and blackmailers. Those who are less courageous and less honest choose management. It is greed alone that drives managers to spend their days persuading morons to carry out simple tasks, arguing with awkward customers and arrogant bosses, being blamed for everything that goes wrong, being stressed out of their mind and driven to drink, drugs, sleepless nights and an early grave.

It is necessary here to distinguish between managers and entrepreneurs. Entrepreneurs (the English version of this French word is 'undertakers', but this is not used in exactly the same way) also plunder the resources of the earth and society in order to assuage their insatiable greed. But successful entrepreneurs must have flair, imagination and courage; managers need none of these, being as a race cowardly and dull. A manager may thus be defined as an individual with overweening greed who lacks the honesty to be a burglar and the imagination to be an entrepreneur.

The Sin of Greed is therefore an ideal field in which to trap Andrew Buckden, and you must strain every nerve to learn how to use its potential to most devastating effect. You must study the Watchers' reports, and supplement these with your own first-hand observation in order to identify the points on which he is most vulnerable. You must also obtain a thorough and up-to-date theoretical knowledge of the subject. Much work has been done on greed within ICM. In particular, we are indebted to the researches of the brilliant Remuneration Consultant of the MDU, Buttertubs, an agent who owes nothing to nepotism. If you are not already completely familiar with his findings, you must become so. A multi-media learning package supported by weekend sweatshops is available from ICM, and you should register for this at once.

Buttertubs has shown that normal humans wish to earn and possess ten per cent more than they actually have. Less than ten per cent they cannot distinguish; more than ten per cent they cannot conceive. Managers, however, are not normal, and the Buttertubs Rule indicates that, as they are promoted, so their greed increases exponentially. Thus supervisors and junior managers may be satisfied with a promotion or pay rise that gives them a fifteen per cent increase. Middle managers may be prepared to accept twenty per cent without complaint. CEs such as Buckden, however, will expect their remuneration to grow at least twenty-five per cent per year.

It is worth considering why managers should expect to be paid more than others. As Buttertubs has pointed out, logic suggests they should be paid less. Others work harder, require more skill and knowledge, have less convenient hours, are more exposed to the elements, are more tightly controlled, have less interesting jobs, and fewer career opportunities. There can be no doubt that this view is correct, but it serves our purposes to keep it hidden; managers' salaries are the noose by which we are best able to lead them in the direction we wish them to go.

Take, as a simple example, a cinema. The projectionist must be fully trained and highly skilled. He must toil hard and continuously, often in cramped and uncomfortable conditions, to ensure all is working properly and safely. His work will, after a time, become repetitive and routine, and there will be no opportunity for him to break out, physically or mentally. If anything goes wrong, he must put it right, and will be held responsible. He will work whatever hours the cinema is open, possibly on shifts. His chances of promotion or any form of career development are probably non-existent.

The manager, on the other hand, will have little to do on most days but stand around and smile at customers. He will have a comfortable office in which to sit or snooze. He will need no identifiable skills. He will be able to wander into town on some vague pretext that no one can question if he gets bored. He will probably be able to claim expenses. He will have opportunities for promotion to posts with even less pressure and better rewards. It is therefore logical that the projectionist should be paid substantially more than the cinema manager, and the same is true of virtually every other industry.

As another example, we may take an engineering company. Its success will depend on the plagiarism of its designers, the fantasies of its marketing experts, the insolence of its salespeople and the cunning of its accountants. To these experts, its managers will have nothing to contribute, except to interfere and obstruct their work. So far from being paid more than them, there must be a serious question why they are employed at all.

There are two interesting spin-offs from the question of managers' salaries, both relating to secrecy. We have imbued UK CEs within the private sector with the conviction that they must do everything within their power to keep the level of their remuneration secret. In consequence, mistrust and suspicion can be stirred up, and colleagues on exactly the same salary can be led into a situation of rivalry and bitter antagonism. Read again the techniques I advised in the Sin of Politicking.

Our approach within the public sector is the opposite. Here, the salary scales are published and it is usually possible to calculate everyone's salary to within a few pence. As a result, most civil servants and local government officers spend much of their 'working' day comparing their remuneration with that of their colleagues. The record for this is held by staff of the Accounts Department of the People's Republic of Chipping Sodbury then under the care of a younger Berepper. During the month of November 1983, 63.5 per cent of their time was spent discussing salaries and grading structure. (Of the remainder, 19.15 per cent went on telling rate-payers the office was unable to answer telephone queries until after 3pm, 11.7

per cent on drinking tea, and 4.9 per cent on telling ratepayers the office was closed for auditing after 3.15pm.)

Buckden, of course, is a Chief Executive, and you must learn how his remuneration is arranged. No one is supposed to know who controls the remuneration of the Chief Executive. In fact, it is usually in the hands of a so-called 'independent' committee. It is an amusing exercise, often used in training Junior Tempters, to trace the various methods by which such a committee is guided to the required conclusion. I imagine you will have completed this during your first term at ICM.

Buckden's remuneration is controlled in this way. The independent committee deciding his salary is appointed by the Board of the United Group. Buckden has been a member of the Board for several years. He and his wife are on visiting terms with them all. Two were at his university, one at his school, and five are members of his club. All but three are members of the same supposedly secret society. The three members of the sub-committee are paid a retainer by the Board for their work. Buckden happened to meet one who was in the company of his mistress in Brussels. A second is suspected of having been discovered some years ago engaging in an unsavoury practice behind the executive bicycle sheds.

Buckden's salary is determined annually by a formula agreed by the Board as a whole. Our agents have not yet learnt what this is; one of your first tasks will be to find it out. However, many such formulae are known to or were developed by us, and Buttertubs has described their operation. Their aim, of course, is to ensure that, whatever happens to the organization, to its shareholders, to the salaries of other workers in it or outside, or to the economy as a whole, the remuneration of the Chief Executive is raised annually by a large amount. We have engineered the introduction of such formulae into all recently-privatized industries with enormous success.

The key to such formulae is the choice of criteria. No obvious measure, such as crude profitability, could produce the desired result. Choice must therefore be made from those that will do so, and the choice must be changed quickly and surreptitiously as conditions vary. Criteria that have proved effective in appropriate circumstances include:

- actual inflation during the past year
- anticipated inflation during the coming year
- reduction in size of workforce
- increase in number of staff controlled
- pay increases paid to the workforce
- pay increases denied to the workforce
- diversification of the organization's activities
- specialization on the organization's core activities
- increase in productivity
- the pay of other chief executives (who are paid more)

It is usually possible to select criteria which will do the necessary.

We have arranged for the pay of Senior Executives below Buckden's level (SEs) to be fixed by the approach known as 'payment by results'. This is similar, but must be geared so that the size of increases is appropriately less, as required by the Buttertubs Rule (see above). Increases must still, of course, be substantially greater than those of the people who actually generate the wealth – the rest of the workforce.

Apart from actual salary level (both CEs and SEs would rather be seen walking down Oxford Street in their underclothes than be paid 'wages') the most important scope for greed is what used to be known as 'perks', but is now referred to as 'payment in kind', 'the package' or, in the building trade, as 'the lump'. Greed can be stimulated almost endlessly by suitable combinations of these items. There are a number of fairly boring, standard elements, such as life insurance, pension, morning coffee and afternoon tea, subsidized mortgage, free health care for the employee, his family, his grandparents and his mistress (if male – female SEs rarely have mistresses, and seem less interested in sex than their male counterparts), use of company flats in London, Paris, or New York, free telephones in house, car and flats, season ticket subsidies, and, of course, entertainment allowances. The relative values attached to these may sometimes surprise you. Most SEs, for example, rate their company car far higher than comprehensive health cover for themselves, partner and children.

Share option schemes, pioneered by Buttertubs some time ago, are a great favourite with CEs. Even hardened Tempters who have not previously met them often find it difficult to believe the sheer cheek of the scheme. Only someone with the instinctive understanding of senior managers' psychology which Buttertubs possesses would have dared to believe it could be accepted. Quite simply, executive share option schemes work by giving CEs the right to buy a given number of their organization's shares at today's prices at any time in the future. Assuming that they have then risen in price (something that continuing inflation virtually guarantees) they can then sell at what is usually a massive profit. In originally floating the concept, Buttertubs made much of the argument that such a scheme would provide an incentive to improve the performance of the company. You will see at once how specious this argument is, as the performance of a company is only one, comparatively minor, element in the price of its shares. In fact, the scheme is an almost perfect way for CEs to enhance each other's remuneration; its value is unknown to their subordinates; it does not figure on the Annual accounts provided for shareholders; it has the tax authorities baffled.

Buttertubs has been working for some time on variations of the scheme. An obvious starting point is the option to buy the company's products at today's prices in the future. However, whilst this might be of interest to CEs of, say a supermarket chain, I doubt if the prospect of buying limitless quantities of garden gnomes would attract Sir Andrew. Resale would also undermine United's own pricing policy. I think Buttertubs is on to a loser here.

The real fun comes by inspiring your manager to invent and make ever more preposterous requests. Buttertubs produced a checklist, which is an invaluable starting point for this. It includes:

- evening dress subsidy
- gardening allowance
- marriage guidance allowance
- subsidized membership of Alcoholics Anonymous
- free psycho-analysis
- guard-dog expenses
- butler's clothing allowance

Payment is not, of course, confined to the period of employment, and greed can be stimulated by what is offered either before or afterwards. You will have learnt by heart the table of statutory British redundancy payments, for which the current maximum is £6,500.46 (for employees who have been employed by the same organization in a senior post from the age of fourteen until retirement at 65). You will also know that the maximum payment in proved cases of wrongful dismissal is £8,500. You may not know that the average leaving payment for SEs is £335,000. Should they be dismissed for a serious dereliction of duty such as allowing their company to be taken over by a rival, or leading it into receivership, the average compensation rises to over £450,000. These payments have long been known by the euphonious name of 'golden handshakes'. This will not be of immediate relevance in your handling of Buckden, but you should bear it in mind.

A more recent development of this theme, for which I claim some little credit, is the invention of the 'golden hallo'. This is a large, lump-sum payment or bribe made at the start of employment. It differs from the golden handshake in that the recipient of the golden hallo has not yet had the opportunity to prove his or her incompetence. It may be paid in kind – the most frequent option being a car. In 1989, I arranged for a young man from Barking to be given golden hallos by seven unit trust companies and three insurance brokers within six months. In each case, he chose a Porsche sports car. Unfortunately, he was an unusually dangerous driver, and crashed each within a few days of receipt.

We are now working on the further, exciting variation which I have already referred to called the 'Golden Gravy Train' (GGT). This has become a key element of the ICM's New Strategy. One aspect of this is that employers will be encouraged to provide their CEs with suitable payments in kind at regular intervals in recognition of each blunder made. This is based on brilliant research by one of our finest agents, widely publicized as the 'Peter Principle'. You will know that this states that managers are promoted up to the level of their incompetence – ie until they are trying to carry out duties that are too difficult for them. I shall have more to say about this when briefing you on the Sixth Deadly Sin – Incompetence. However, it is also of direct relevance to the question of remuneration, and hence of Greed.

GGT relies on the fact that it is easier to promote unsatisfactory managers than to sack them. It may also be cheaper. Once promoted, such managers are well placed to obtain higher grade posts in other organizations, and knowledge of this fact will also encourage existing employers to promote them. Many managers have moved rapidly to the very top of the GGT, thus causing endless damage to all with whom they come into contact. However, GGT is relevant to Buckden only in that he may be tempted to use it for unsatisfactory colleagues. Watch closely for any opportunities. Our boys are working on further variations of the theme. 'Golden handcuffs' are already widely in use. 'Golden bedsocks' are under development.

Love of money was once identified by a prominent member of the Other Side as 'the root of all evil'. Of course he was wrong, but the claim had enough truth to cause us some embarrassment. You will know from your elementary history lesson how we invented money, and the endless destructive uses we have put it to over the centuries. Quite early on, as you will remember, we developed numerous money equivalents, from beads to shrunken heads. By far the most effective of these is the modern invention of credit cards, a device we owe to Glapthorne. The unique advantage of credit cards is their unrivalled power to induce chronic and continuous overspending. This feature alone produces for us a steady and useful crop of bankruptcies, scandals, broken marriages and suicides.

A year or two ago, however, there was a feeling in the minds of some members of the Management Committee of the ICM that Glapthorne's initiative had run its course. The more perceptive users who had been persuaded to obtain three credit cards in case only one was acceptable had gradually realized that where one would do, so would the others, and were actively considering handing one in. The belief was expressed that our funds could do more damage if used in other ways. But Glapthorne's brilliant and characteristic answer was to go on to the attack. Far from retrenching, he persuaded card holders that the more cards they had, the greater the advantage. Every card allowed additional credit. Every card conferred extra prestige when the collection was flashed in wallet or bag. Glapthorne exploited this status value of cards to the full by inventing the Gold Card, and its list of spurious and meaningless benefits. Even more astute was his invention of the debit card. This actually disbenefits users by ensuring that their spending is debited to their account in the shortest possible time, and offers no user advantages whatever. The means by which he promoted this device are amongst the cleverest I have ever seen deployed. Here indeed is a fiend capable of selling hellfire to those living on the slopes of an active volcano.

Glapthorne has now gone one step further. His masterstroke with the debit card enabled him to persuade the Board of ICM to endorse development of its own card. As it is still only being piloted in a limited way, a few basic details will be of interest. It is to be known as the Lucifer Card (Clootie Card in Scotland). It will be available in dirty Green, Gilt and Platinum versions. Each is elegantly designed, with a hologram of the All Lowest in full regalia. The Green card carries a picture of the traditional pawnbroker's sign, the Gilt a fine drawing of the City of London Bankruptcy Court, and the Platinum a contemporary reproduction print of the Fleet Debtor's Prison. At a stroke, Glapthorne combined two of the most powerful sins and created the Greed Club.

Glapthorne's scheme is carefully devised to maximize profit. Only those already owning one debit card and at least two credit cards will be considered. The type of card issued will depend on the level of the applicant's existing card debts; Green for those owing up to £10,000 only, Gilt up to £25,000, and Platinum for those owing above this figure. No applicant who has paid off the full amount owing on an existing card within the interest-free period will be considered. (Our credit-rating agency will check this.)

RECEPTION
AB

A superb range of benefits will be offered to users. These include:

- Free third party insurance for airship travel
- 0.25 per cent discount on diamond tiaras (participating jewellers only)
- Reduced rates for selected services at brothels displaying the card sign
- Preferential booking service for the Lord Mayor's Show
- Free inclusion on over 500 junk mailing lists
- Unitemized statements passed to the cardholder by agreed dead-letter drops

Gilt card holders will qualify for a free plastic hip-flask holster. Platinum card holders will be able to use the No-questions-asked double hotel room booking service. All Lucifer/Clootie cardholders will be credited with points for all card purchases at the rate of 1 for ever £10,000 spent. Those accumulating 100 points within 12 months will receive a congratulatory letter from Glapthorne. The cards are also useful as screw-drivers, for scraping ice off windscreens, wedging rattling windows, spreading butter, cleaning finger nails, and opening Yale-type locks.

You probably wish to ask how the many aspects of remuneration that I have discussed may best be used for managers' destruction. There are many ways; to know of a weakness is to have an opportunity to harm. Managers' greed may be exploited by:

- starvation
- over-feeding
- poisoning
- obsession

Which is most effective depends on the manager's personality type; there are several excellent tests available from

MDU to help establish this, although all are fiendishly expensive, and require special training.

Starvation involves ensuring that the manager's greed is never satisfied - that he is forever hungry. It is thus suitable for the over-ambitious, the envious, the immature, and all who place an unrealistic value on their own abilities. It can prove valuable for destroying newly appointed graduates. It is also appropriate for those with large families or extravagant partners, drug addicts and others with unusual and expensive tastes.

Over-feeding, or paying managers more than they believe they are worth, is a much less usual technique. It can occasionally be effective for managers who suffer from a serious inferiority complex, are particularly conscientious, or hold deep religious convictions. There are, needless to say, hardly any managers in any of these categories. In the right cases, it produces chronic anxiety, continual over-work, and feelings of guilt. Only in the most extreme cases is the excessive remuneration actually refused.

Poisoning is the process of remunerating managers in a way that will harm them. It is easier to arrange in some situations than others. Thus dipsomaniacs can readily be promoted to management positions in the hospitality industry, and heavy smokers in the tobacco trade. But there are far more opportunities than inexperienced Tempters sometimes realize. An executive dining room providing free lunches and midday drinks has, for example, destroyed thousands of managers. I have already mentioned the provision of fast company cars to dangerous drivers. There are many more subtle methods of poisoning which depend on accurate knowledge of the individual manager's weaknesses. Some have been destroyed by the opportunity to visit parts of the world in which sexually-transmitted disease is rife. Occasionally it may even be possible to destroy managers by offering them experimental use of new products being pioneered by their organization - drugs, for example, or ladders.

Obsession is the feeding of a manager's unhealthy and unbalanced beliefs about some aspects of remuneration, analogous to the increasingly faddish and obsessive beliefs we are encouraging about food itself. This is easier to use with remuneration substitutes of the kind I have already mentioned. However, there are a few, unusual situations in which it is helpful with direct remuneration. Thus a manager may believe that his importance in society can only properly be demonstrated by the use of ever bigger and more expensive cars, and accept so much of his remuneration in this form he is unable to meet the needs of his family. This is rarer than you might think, as partners tend to share the same view.

Of course managers are not the only greedy humans. We are steadily improving our techniques for destroying managers through the greed of others. So far, most progress has been made here by Carlton Scroop on the US desk of MDU. He has taken the litigious propensities of Americans as his starting point, and so exploited them that there seems no end to what he will be able to achieve. At first, he confined himself to standard lawsuits for badly designed, defective or incorrectly described goods or services. By stimulating such activity he was able to increase the stress levels of managers measurably. However, he then moved into quite new territory, such as instructions and warnings issued (or not issued).

Perhaps the height of his success so far has been the case in which the purchaser of a bicycle who was injured whilst riding at night without lights successfully sued the manufacturer for failing to warn him against doing this. Scroop is planning what currently looks like an irresistible advance along this line of attack. His 'no win – no fee' legal advisory helpline is now advising clients who wish to sue:

- Fishmongers who fail to provide written notice to all purchasers of the possibly fatal consequences of swallowing large fish bones
- Car makers who fail to warn owners of the dangers of parking on railway crossings
- The manufacturers of clothes lines who do not make clear that if tied round the neck and tightened there is a risk of strangulation
- Undertakers who fail to provide bells within their coffins so that those enclosed prematurely may make their revival known

I suggest you have a quick word with him. He is sure to have suggestions as to how careless and stupid customers can sue United for some harm they have brought upon themselves with their garden gnomes. As a starter, I understand that the house of a customer living in Rayners Lane became almost unsaleable because of the twenty-seven Fishing Gnomes his wife had arranged round the pond inside the front gate. There may be grounds for action against United here, but it will be necessary to ensure that the case is brought in the US; British courts are in this way, as in so many others, behind the times.

This, then, is the next area in which you must tempt Buckden. Up to last year, his greed was satisfied. The competition from ICC has ensured that this has not continued. Increasing desire for the unattainable is in any case characteristic of the ageing process in humans. Play on this weakness by every means at your disposal. Leave reports of what other Chief Executives are paid where he will see them. Plant the belief in his mind that Smithers must have a package worth at least twice as much as his own. Prompt his wife to talk of the many things she does not have. Get his daughter to remind him of her forthcoming wedding. Suggest to his son that a fast and expensive sports car would enhance both his career and his marriage prospects. Point out to Buckden that Smithers races an ocean-going yacht and others have founded world-famous art collections, or even endowed colleges. Get friends to introduce him to the life of the casino. Let him look in the mirror and wonder how long he may have to enjoy the fruits of his labours. It is all easier than you think. Above all keep ICC's success and its effect on his pocket and pride continuously in his mind. Ensure that he meets Smithers frequently. With only a little ingenuity, this should prove the basis for his ultimate destruction.

This is the watershed, nephew. I look forward eagerly to reports of your early success.

Your ever-loving Uncle

Barripper

Instrument 5: GREED

INSTRUCTIONS

Choose one option for each statement. Whatever happens, eternal damnation is bound to follow.

1. Your future development hinges on
   a) your efforts
   b) your qualifications
   c) your background and pedigree
   d) your contacts

2. You would expect your benefits package to include
   a) a handsome portfolio of unpaid shares
   b) membership of the Reform Club
   c) a secure non-contributable pension
   d) ten weeks' paid holiday

3. Pay increases are
   a) a matter of confidentiality
   b) a tool for maintaining the status quo
   c) a source of mystery
   d) no longer important

4. Redundancy holds no fears because
   a) of knowledge of your golden bedsocks

b) of the secret files you have compiled on the Board

c) of your contacts and directorships

d) you know it means a higher salary

5. Corporate liquidity is the result of

a) knowing how to balance the books

b) industrial espionage

c) taking the rough with the smooth

d) a healthy financial reserve

6. Pay decreases are

a) a method of squeezing out the vestiges of worker resistance

b) a method of gaining a higher pay rise

c) a method of gaining social credibility

d) an unnecessary evil

7. Government benefits are

a) a canker to be erased

b) a windfall for department budgets

c) a prop for others

d) a drain on the economy

8. The Futures market is

a) a source of mystery

b) a pot of gold

c) too great a risk

d) for the destruction of upstarts

9. Tax-deductions are
   a) a thing of the past
   b) an annual budget sop
   c) job provision for accountants
   d) irrelevant

10. The key to real power lies in
   a) your personal organizer
   b) controlling your time
   c) a seat in the House of Lords
   d) loadsacash

SCORING

1.	a 1	b 2	c 5	d 8
2.	a 9	b 7	c 2	d 4
3.	a 7	b 6	c 0	d 10
4.	a 10	b 8	c 8	d 10
5.	a 7	b 4	c 0	d 3
6.	a 2	b 8	c 6	d 0
7.	a 8	b 0	c 4	d 0
8.	a 0	b 6	c 0	d 6
9.	a 1	b 1	c 1	d 6
10.	a 3	b 3	c 6	d 10

ANALYSIS

65+: your single-mindedness is the envy of all who shun you. Your transparent lust for more is a shining example to the ambitious and a killer-blow to the altruistic. You trample others underfoot on the way to the bank.

30–64: it is difficult to know whether

a) you are just not trying hard enough
b) you cleverly conceal your naked ambitions
c) you want to go the whole hog
d) your overdrawn bank account is a source of mystery.

Under 30: Shame. You must be extremely greedy but just no good at it.

Chapter 6

Incompetence

'There is a demand these days for men who can make wrong appear right.'

TERENCE

My dear Relubbus

The news you give me gets better by the day. That, spurred on by jealousy of Smithers, he should have persuaded his Board to grant him a 120 per cent increase in salary plus a 'performance' bonus related only to the total number of gnomes produced is worthy not so much of the CE of a privatized industry as of a senior member of an old-style politbureau. The unfavourable comment it has already brought forth from a couple of his non-executive directors is nothing to the public outcry that will rapidly ensue. Congratulations! This time, Buckden will not escape our grasp. I am, for the first time, looking forward to your annual appraisal; I feel certain that an appropriate decrease - possibly as low as 10 per cent – may be justified.

I was dining last week with the Archtempter responsible for staff appointments. He tells me that a posting to undertake the destruction of a Board member of a multi-national oil and soft drinks conglomerate is coming up.

However, we must not become complacent. No war is won until the last battle. The next stage in your destruction of Sir Andrew Buckden (I can never restrain a chuckle at his new 'handle') is the juiciest yet. We have now arrived at the sixth of the Deadly Sins of Management –

The Sin of Incompetence. Like some of the others, this often surprises Trainee Tempters when they first meet it. 'Surely,' they say, 'whatever else we can lay at the door of senior managers, they must at least be competent in their job? How else can they have got there?' This, of course, is before they participate in the seminar on the Peter Principle, the inspired idea of one of the most celebrated of our double agents, which I mentioned when telling you about the Deadly Sin of Greed. This states the almost self-evident truth that managers are promoted only as long as they are doing a good job – ie up to the level of their incompetence. It has two corollaries; all managers must inevitably end in a job they do badly, and the more senior the manager, the more certain he or she is to be incompetent. We deliberately allowed the leaking of this Principle in order to undermine subordinates' respect for their bosses; it has done a good job for us.

But the Peter Principle also suggests that until they have reached their 'level of incompetence', managers are likely to do their job well. This is, of course, a serious misconception, although a common one. A survey carried out recently by first-year students in the Management School of the University of Pinner (formerly an Evening Extension Class of Harrow Tech [Pinner branch]) showed that, of the representative sample surveyed, only 4 per cent were thoroughly competent and 17 per cent fairly competent, whilst 29 per cent were fairly incompetent, and a full 50 per cent were thoroughly incompetent. These results have been challenged from two directions. It has been objected that the sample contained too high a proportion of local government officers and garage managers, thus overstating incompetence. On the other hand, it was also suggested that the exclusion of the 'don't knows' had skewed the results towards competence. I think we can safely accept that any deficiencies in the survey were mutually contradictory, and that the level of managerial incompetence has been proved to be satisfactorily high.

Other studies support this common-sense conclusion. Wormhill showed that, of three hundred and thirty-eight executive Board members surveyed:

- 98 per cent never read agenda or briefing papers before a Board meeting had actually started, and 91 per cent never even glanced at them during the meeting
- 88 per cent could make neither head nor tail of their monthly budget printout
- 65 per cent were unable to remember the names of more than half their direct subordinates
- 29 per cent had failed to attend at least one crucial appointment within the previous week
- The Chief Executives of 76 per cent were desperate to find an excuse for removing them
- The secretaries of 99.4 per cent were desperate to work for someone else
- 71 per cent could not organize a knees-up in a brewery, even when provided with a comprehensive checklist and an electronic orgy organizer

Suggestive as these findings are, this is no more than the tip of the iceberg.

It is commonly believed that the worst examples of incompetence are to be found in the public sector. Whether or not this is true depends on how incompetence is measured. Whilst money is the commonest measure, a number of others have been suggested. Wormhill suggests *number of lives lost* (as the result of decisions intended to achieve something else; if the decision was intended to cause death, the converse measure is used). Based on the standard deviation of the totals killed, he rates 'supreme incompetence' as the direct loss of at least 1 million lives. This has been achieved by only seventeen people, of whom sixteen were senior officers in the First World War. The seventeenth was a well-known brewer.

A more generally useful measure of incompetence has been developed by the recently-promoted Droomer. Droomer has postulated that the best measure of incompetence is what he has dubbed 'the timespan of consequent obsolescence' (TCO). Droomer's approach is to measure the number of person days of those affected elapsing between the manager's attention first being drawn to a matter and the final outcome. Typical results he has calculated include:

A manager unable to locate a set of vital papers he had taken with him on an overseas trip:

> TCO = 1.5 (0.5 days × 3 people, based on the time he, his secretary and the subordinate he accused of losing them spent searching)

A manager who delayed a necessary office move affecting 250 staff for 18 months:

> TCO = 136,875 (1.5 years × 365 days × 250 people affected)

A planning committee taking five years to finalize its decision on a new hospital:

> TCO = 182,500,000 (5 × 365 × 100,000 people)

The delay in building the rail link between the English mouth of the Channel Tunnel and London:

> TCO = 730,000,000,000 (20 years × 365 days × 100,000,000 people)

Useful as money, delay and lives lost are as quick measures of incompetence, they are, of course, not the only ones. The results of top management incompetence are everywhere to be seen. You will probably remember the board on the wall of the entrance hall of ICM listing some of its alumni's greatest achievements; world-famous names who, under our guidance, led their troops to disaster. Two earthly management authors wrote a book a few years ago called *In Search of Excellence*. It described in glowing terms the philosophies of a number of companies and how they achieved success. Within a short space of earthly time, many of these were in serious difficulties. Indeed, there is often so little time between success and failure that those involved have not received the 'honours' heaped on them by a grateful country before their organization has failed.

Commission of any and all of the Seven Deadly Sins can be seen in each failure. But it is this Sixth Sin, of sheer incompetence that I now urge you to consider. Bad design, inadequate development and testing of new products, unbalanced product ranges, failure to anticipate market changes or competitors' moves, overtrading, uncontrolled and over-rapid expansion, lack of basic cost control, the list is endless. The most junior manager, just promoted to his first management post, could spot the errors and would know how to avoid them. Do not yet dismiss our knight of the gnomes; there may still be glimmers of the younger Buckden left.

How, then, have we induced experienced managers to commit such follies? It is perhaps here more than at any other point that the differences between ordinary and brilliant Tempters is demonstrated. The crucial area, of course, is the manager's decision-making process; it is this you must understand, and use for his destruction.

There are numerous fancy and unbelievably complex 'decision-making processes' taught in management schools. Naturally none of these is, or could be, used in real life. In fact, senior managers make decisions in one of three basic ways, depending on their philosophy of life; they are either autocratic, democratic or cowardly. Each requires a different approach by the Tempter.

Autocratic managers are great fun, and much the easiest to deal with. Their concern is exclusively with *what to do*; they decide what they want, and then do it. They make no attempt to analyse situations, and they despise those who do. They have such mottoes as:

'Don't just sit there – do something.'
'When the going gets tough, the tough get going.'
'Don't confuse me with the facts – my mind's made up.'

In their rush to join us, they ride roughshod over both people or facts that get in their way; there is usually little or no need for our intervention. Their incompetence often remains hidden for a surprisingly long time, especially from those closest to them. The key is to ensure that the manager makes up his mind instantly, and gives his subordinates only insufficient hints as to what he wants them to recommend. Achingill's module from the Two Day Advanced Tempters' refresher workshop illustrates the techniques to perfection. The brief for students is:

> It is suggested that the government Department of Information Technology, with a staff of 1,000, should be relocated from London to Moreton-in-Marsh, where a large country house in extensive grounds (previously used as a mental hospital) has become available. Prepare suitable submissions and financial cases on the assumptions (A) that the secretary of States *wants* to move, and (B) that he *does not want* to move.

The model answer for Case A is:
Moreton-in-Marsh Hall is a large house of great history and character; a Grade 1 listed building in extensive grounds with ample room for expansion. It has numerous outbuildings, and is near the delightful Cotswold market town from which it takes its name. There is cheap housing within commuting distance. The station is served by direct fast trains to London, and the M40 motorway is nearby. Wage levels in the area are substantially lower than in London, and London allowances are not payable. The financial effect of the move will be:

COSTS

	£
Purchase of property	500,000
Removal of furniture, equipment etc	100,000
Necessary refurbishments & redecoration	50,000
Total (non-recurring) costs	£650,000

ANNUAL SAVINGS

	£
Reduction in annual salary/wages costs	1,000,000
Reduction in rates	50,000
Total (annual) savings	£1,050,000

The model answer for Case B is:
Moreton-in-Marsh Hall is a grandiose house in large, neglected grounds. The property will require much adaptation, and as a Grade 1 listed building, planning permission will present problems. The numerous outbuildings are in a poor state of repair, and many are fit only for demolition. The nearby town is partly dormitory suburb and partly weekend retreat; local labour is difficult

to obtain and largely unskilled. The only supplies of available housing within practicable commuting distance are in Swindon and Oxford, both over thirty miles away. Transport is difficult, with only one direct train to London daily, and the M40 motorway suffers chronic overcrowding and delays. The financial effect of the move will be:

COSTS

	£
Purchase of property	500,000
Removal of furniture, equipment etc	100,000
Relocation allowances for staff	500,000
Necessary refurbishments & redecoration	500,000
Telecommunications costs	500,000
Demolition of outbuildings	50,000
Fire and safety requirements	750,000
Car park and roadways	100,000
Recruitment, training and redundancy costs	2,000,000
Total costs	£5,000,000

ADDITIONAL ANNUAL EXPENDITURE

	£
Increased travel and transport costs	100,000
Increased maintenance cost	100,000
Total additional annual expenditure	£200,000

Of course neither proposal will bear any resemblance to what will actually happen.

If the move is made, the staff unions will refuse to cooperate, and most of the staff will have to be relocated to specially-created posts in the London area. It will prove impossible to relet the present London building which, after lying empty in a steadily deteriorating state for six years will have to be demolished. A serious structural fault resulting from an underground stream will render parts of Moreton-in-Marsh Hall too dangerous for use, and staff in the remaining section will complain about ghostly noises and the appearance of a disembodied head.

If the move is not made, new legislation will require an increase of 750 staff within the year. Attempts to accommodate these within the existing building will result in dangerous over-crowding and a prolonged official strike. The overspill will eventually be located at Chipping Ongar, leading to chronic communication and travel problems. To overcome the increasing difficulty of recruiting office staff in the London area, a sophisticated computer network will be introduced. This will prove incapable of meeting its specification, and work will have to be subcontracted at immense expense to private agencies in Heckmondwyke and Cockermouth.

Democratic decision makers use words such as 'participation', 'commitment' and 'ownership'. They are more concerned with *how* a decision is made, than what it is; indeed, they feel it is wrong to try to impose their own wishes and require different and somewhat more subtle techniques. Look back at some of my previous advice when you were tackling the younger Buckden, especially the letter on creativity. I am sure that Buckden will be more susceptible now to furnishing his subordinates with the true rewards of their ownership.

I will not dwell on those who refrain from decision-making through **cowardice**. The report on your retraining gave an excellent account of your prowess in this area. In any event, we agree that Buckden would not submit easily to a campaign of this kind.

The ICM has sought to nourish incompetence in many ways. Some years ago, it introduced the annual Bad Design Awards. These are in three classes, bronze, silver and gold. Originally, the Awards were for household equipment and took the form of miniature bread toasters which could be plugged in and used. Their electronic programming was designed to reproduce the effects of the real thing; according to a random and unpredictable sequence, bread was either burnt black (all over or in selected areas), remained completely untoasted, or became jammed inside. The awards therefore became known as 'Crummies'. The first was won by the Cafetière with a domed lid to ensure coffee spillage.

The scope of the Awards was gradually widened, although in the past, complaints were frequently made that the judging was biased. For over a decade, the gold Awards were won exclusively by the architectural profession. The succession of tower blocks and office buildings they entered in the sixties and seventies proved unbeatable. During the eighties they met serious competition from the computer industry. The Golden Crummy for 1985 was won outright by the six hundred and fifty page users' manual provided with a popular PCW; its masterly incomprehensibility persuaded over half those purchasing to abandon the use of computers permanently. In 1990, the judges had no hesitation in making the award to a prominent software company for its new word-processing package. In the words of the citation:

> This package demonstrates bad design of an original and subtle kind. Its customer-unfriendliness is achieved by the simple technique of *adding unwanted features*. What might thus have been in danger of being an efficient and useful tool has been reduced to a baffling complexity that is ably supported by a lengthy, superfluously worded and totally unreadable manual.

Recently the road transport industry has moved into first place with such nominations as:

- Seat-belts with automatic jamming to prevent any movement whatever
- Pedestrian controlled lights that change when all pedestrians crossed three minutes ago and the then empty road has filled with heavy traffic in both directions (These won nomination by a short head over traffic lights that keep cars waiting for 5 minutes at an empty junction)
- Dashboard shelves which slide objects to an inaccessible slot towards the door
- Car interior lights placed immediately behind the driver's head

This year's nominations include the European Commission (for the unusability of their forms), BSI (for BS5750), and of course the Citizen's Charter (as evidence that the written word bears no significance whatsoever).

I can now reveal to you the very latest work to come out of the ICM, embodying the thinking of the superb young team of recently-recruited ex staff of the British Department of Trade and Industry. Under the leadership of Burntisland, they have developed a new structure of qualification based on incompetence. Through suitable pressure on their ex-colleagues, they have arranged for the establishment of the National Council for Incompetence-based Qualifications (NCIQ). They are known as National Incompetence Qualifications (NIQs) (except in Rutland; Rutland Incompetence Qualifications [RIQs] are identical, but have been developed by the Academic Board of the University of Morcott and Barrowden sitting as the Rutland Council for Incompetence-based Qualifications [RCIQ]). Neither qualification is recognized outside its respective area.

Burntisland's team were able to demonstrate the positive correlation between incompetence and promotion. They found three reasons for this. The first I have already referred to – the well-known 'Peter Principle'. The second they dubbed the 'Burntisland Effect'. This states that there is natural reluctance to allow competent workers to move or be promoted; thus, ambitious workers are strongly motivated to display incompetence. The third reason for the value of incompetence they have called the 'Law of Maximum Visibility'. This is based on the observation that the greater a worker's skill, the less obvious it is; thus the more incompetent the worker, the more he or she is noticed.

The NCIQ qualifications have been extensively promoted by grants from the Cultural Fund of the EU, and their use in countries of the former Eastern Bloc is being encouraged with the UK 'Show-How' Fund. The RCIQ has received financial support from the EU Regional Development Fund, and its qualifications are being used as a model for vocational training in parts of the Mekong Delta and the left bank of the White Nile. The funds are used in three ways; to ensure that the pay of the senior staff of the Councils remains competitive; to provide regular employment for consultants on the Councils' Approved Register; and to bribe employers to force their staff to obtain the qualifications.

There are six levels of incompetence. Level 1 is at operative level. It is already extensively used in the catering and public transport industries. Its possession indicates that the holder is capable of the degree of rudeness and carelessness required for their posts. Level 6 is still under development. It will apply to directors, civil servants of grade 8 and above, and senior professionals. The holder will have demonstrated a high degree of skills including arrogance, blindness to the obvious, and pig-headed obstinacy about the rightness of their own beliefs.

The process of assessment for NIQs is necessarily complex and expensive, designed as it is to keep large numbers of well-paid but otherwise unemployable people at work. We advised Pinner to use our own processes as a model, and this they have done and done well.

In particular, the application of APL (Alien Profitable Logic) is ingenious. Before APL the qualification or requalification of Tempters could only be achieved by sitting and passing a series of difficult examinations. This, of course, made it difficult for senior members of the Lowerarchy (such as myself) to ensure that those they wished to succeed did so, whilst those they wished to fail could duly be held back. With the coming of APL, however, control has been fully established. As with the method of 'continuous assessment' we have installed in many earthly schools, we can now ensure that the teachers of those we favour will mark them high, and of those we dislike will mark them low. The degree of control this has given us is most satisfying. Your own spell of retraining was, I have to inform you, reduced by 133 years thanks to my personal involvement in your APL. My invoice is attached.

APL has been fully adapted to the assessment of N/RIQs. Burntisland's team also had available the model of our own Infernal Assessment Centre (IAC), and this has formed a basis for their work with the N/RCIQs. You may not yet be familiar with the IAC, although it will play an important role in your future. Its use is to assess promising Tempters and provide a profile for use when filling senior posts within the Lowerarchy. A brief description of its modus operandi will, I think, be not only interesting but useful to you.

The IAC is located in the remains of a once impregnable castle on the island of Foula off the west coast of Shetland. This location was chosen for a number of reasons. Getting there is in itself a test of ingenuity and persistence. Once there, escape is difficult. The building and surroundings offer scope for numerous tests. The Director of Assessment, MacGhillicuddy Reeks, always fancied himself as a Scottish Laird, and relishes the ambience.

The programme of the IAC lasts for three days. Tempters who make it to the Centre are allocated to teams of six on arrival. They are required to wear top hats in the colour of their team, and bearing their individual number. Their rooms are located either in the roofless North Wing or the incomplete Stable Court. The rooms, lavatories and the Grand Hall in which testees eat are fully wired for sound; the tapes are used in assessment, for blackmail, or to supplement the income of the Director by sale to the richer and more sensible testees. The main elements in the programme are:

The T-Group (T = tasteless). In this test, teams of testees are locked in a dark unheated room, without explanation or guidance, for four hours. During this time, testees involuntarily reveal their basic personality types. The hypochondriacs complain, the ingenious suggest amusing ways of passing the time, the lascivious make suggestive comments or commit indecent assaults, the aggressive commit acts of aggression on the passive, who become victims. Those who come out alive and in possession of some degree of sanity pass on to the next test.

The whisky tasting. This occurs at lunch on the first full day, and usually comes as a surprise to testees. Its aim is three-fold; to establish whether testees possess the social skills necessary to be credible in senior dining rooms; to find out how much liquor they can hold; and to provide Reeks with an excuse for indulgence. Testees unable to distinguish the house whisky (distilled from locally-collected sea-weed at 98% proof by Reeks himself) from a commercially available blend are immediately (a) stoned and (b) failed.

Hunting the haggis. In setting up teams, testees have been divided into those who know the truth about haggis and those who do not. The team of the ignorant is provided with cross-bows, belts hung with dead capercalie, and bagpipes. They are told that haggis eat capercalie, are attracted by the sound of the bagpipes, have three toes, walk backwards, and make a curious wailing noise. Their task is to go forth and return with at least one dead haggis. The team of the knowledgeable is provided with boots that make three-toed, backward facing tracks and horns that produce a curious wailing noise. They are told to lure the ignorant as far as possible into the local peat bogs. It is unusual for more than half the members of either team to return from this exercise. Those that do continue to the next test.

The psychiatrist's interviews. These are conducted on a one-to-one basis at hourly intervals throughout the first night in a room at the top of the garden tower. After a quiet, conventional opening, during which the testee is subjected to questions suggesting he is either homosexual or has committed incest, the psychiatrist suddenly leaps towards the window, shouting 'That's it! I can't stand any more! Another heterosexual fiend! I've had enough!' and makes to open the window to jump out. The reaction of the testee is recorded on video; those who try to prevent the apparent suicide are failed; those who watch with an interested smile go forward with high marks. There is normally a large trampoline beneath the window, although this has occasionally been removed for use by one of the teams on the all-night exercise. Fortunately, we are particularly well stocked with psychiatrists.

The first team exercise. After dinner on the first full day, the teams are briefed for the first major exercise. They are told that their object is to recover the recipe for a newly-invented design of beefburger which was entered into the memory of a notebook computer that was stolen by an industrial spy disguised as a Slovakian birdwatcher who was last seen by an old fisherman wandering on the shore in the extreme west of the island on the day following the celebration of Up-Helly-Aa. Beyond this, they are told nothing except that the return boat leaves for the mainland in forty-eight hours' time. Their equipment consists of three tins of prunes, a set of cricket pads, a street map of Cheltenham and parts from an old cuckoo clock.

Most teams begin by trying to bribe the Dean of Outdoor Studies, Knockando. His response is to hold an auction, after which he conducts the team making the highest bid into an old pigsty on the home farm and locks them in. The next move varies. Some teams make tracks towards the west coast of the island, with the idea of locating the old fisherman and offering prunes in exchange for information. Other seek the ferryman, to enquire who has recently left or arrived on Foula. A few attempt to break into the Senior Common Room to find the paperwork for the exercise, but the most intelligent set about trying to contact members of previous courses. They find, however, that the only telephone on the island is located at the end of the pier in a box now used for storing fishing nets, and functions only on old pennies.

The exercise has never been completed, and teams are judged by the originality of the size of the bribes they offer.

Group creativity. This exercise starts at 0500 on the second day. Teams are shown the remains of the former ice-house in the castle grounds. This consists of a dank, cave-like hole in the side of artificial mound, lined with dripping, slime-covered stonework. Bats hang from the roof, rats can be heard scurrying about the floor, and rotting and foul-smelling vegetation is heaped in the corners. Teams are asked to devise a scheme for the commercial exploitation of the ice-house, and to prepare fully-costed proposals and a business plan for presentation to the Director and Academic Board at 1100. They are also told the ice-house is a Grade 1 listed building.

Psychometric testing. The afternoon of Day 2 is spent in completion of a battery of psychometric tests. The first is the well-known MDUI instrument. This is based on Achingill's research into the toilet-training methods of the Magutsi tribe in Papua New Guinea, which revealed thirty-two combinations of mother-child interaction. The results were validated against control groups of Yale sophomores during the first year of the Vietnam War. There has been some discussion of the relevance and predictive value of the test in the selection of Tempters. However as, apart from his unassailable international reputation, Achingill is known to be a close friend of the All Lowest Himself, it is now universally accepted that the value of the test is very high.

Other tests are designed to establish testees' extraversion, intraversion and aversion to answering stupid questions; their ability to cheat; their facility for turning diagrams of oddly-shaped patterns inside out whilst counting backwards to a hundred, and other essential life skills. The complete battery is widely regarded as one of the most exhausting in use anywhere, and has been the subject of papers at many international colloquia. It also fills a rather awkward slot in the programme.

The final exercise for the few testees who remain begins at 1700. The brief is to circumnavigate the island by land, obtaining specified objects from a number of points as proof of attainment. These points include the inner chamber of a sea cave, accessible only along a thirty-foot submerged passage; the summit of a sheer 250-foot sea stack; and a stone-age burial chamber. The final point is on the island of Unst, where testees have to obtain the signature of the keeper of the lighthouse at Muckle Flugger. As this last objective involves outwitting the RAF commandant, it is unusual for there to be more than a handful of survivors. Its relevance to the duties of Senior Tempter has occasionally been questioned. Directly, it has none. Indirectly, it reflects the typical basis for much earthly management selection, and thus those who do well in it are able to enter into the minds of their charges to be.

As no testee has ever made it beyond Day 2, the programme for the third day is still under development.

In my enthusiasm for these developments I have allowed myself to digress. I think you need little advice at this stage. However, there is one potentially explosive development to which I must draw your attention. A report from a prominent double agent employed in the Press Office of the British Prime Minister appears to suggest that the names of those to receive life peerages in the imminent 'Honours' list include that of Buckden. There is a possibility that the code has been misread; I am having it checked, and will let you have the result as soon as possible.

I look forward to your next report with keen anticipation.

Your loving Uncle

Barripper

Instrument 6: INCOMPETENCE

INSTRUCTIONS

Merely select one option of those presented. For example, if you think that 'Wind Power is fundamental to the future of mankind' is your preferred statement, select option c.

1. Wind power is
   a) an idealist's dream
   b) a source of mystery
   c) fundamental to the future of mankind
   d) irrelevant

2. Football is
   a) the major cause of gang warfare
   b) the opium of the masses
   c) a source of mystery
   d) for people who won't grow up

3. Having in-laws to stay is
   a) something to look forward to
   b) irksome
   c) an opportunity to work late
   d) a source of mystery

4. Pruning shrubs in autumn
   a) stunts their growth
   b) stunts your growth
   c) improves the value of your property
   d) will secure the return of the Labour Party

5. Snow clearance in winter is something
   a) to make you emigrate
   b) to observe from a distance
   c) for which we are ill-equipped
   d) to do in winter

6. Synchronized swimming
   a) is a growth leisure activity
   b) is for somebody else
   c) is a source of mystery
   d) is soporific

7. A creaking door
   a) is no hassle when shut
   b) needs a spot of oil
   c) is worth two in the bush
   d) is a portent of things to come

8. Propagating your own plants from seed
   a) ruins the economy
   b) makes you fit

c) is the act of a perverse mind
d) is a source of new plants

9. A pipe-rack on the wall
    a) is a demonstration of will power
    b) needs dusting
    c) is a source of intense pleasure
    d) is worth two in the bush

10. Figures in public life
    a) had a terrible childhood
    b) are a source of mystery
    c) are good for TV commercials
    d) refuse to grow up

SCORING

1.	a 2	b 0	c 0	d 10
2.	a 4	b 10	c 8	d 8
3.	a 2	b 0	c 0	d 10
4.	a 4	b 10	c 6	d 0
5.	a 0	b 10	c 7	d 0
6.	a 3	b 10	c 2	d 6
7.	a 8	b 6	c 5	d 0
8.	a 10	b 10	c 10	d 10
9.	a 10	b 0	c 4	d 0
10.	a 0	b 0	c 10	d 0

ANALYSIS

70 and above: you have succeeded in pushing incompetence to a new high. Your belief in your own

self-importance should see you all the way to the top and cause untold damage.

40–70: not trying nearly hard enough. You may be on the verge of a breakthrough, but are yet to do any real damage.

Under 40: not good enough. You are not incompetent enough to rise to the top and will probably continue to accomplish mundane tasks with a high degree of effectiveness.

Chapter 7
Corruption

'Power corrupts, but lack of power corrupts absolutely.'

My dear Relubbus

So! Sir Andrew is in line for a life peerage! This ultimate dissolution is testimony to the skill with which I have directed his case and also, of course, to the obedience with which you have carried out my instructions. But we must leave no doubt about the totality of his destruction, and the seventh and final Deadly Sin of Management – *The Sin of Corruption* – will ensure this.

'Honest managers' is not a class that many ambitious executives rush to join. Try the description out on a class of MBA students, and watch the wry smiles and tight lips.

A major element in corruption is, of course, the bribe. Honest managers do not offer, or accept bribes. This statement appears so clear, so absolute, that Trainee Tempters often believe that the area is barren. Nothing could be further from the truth. Almost every word in the statement is open to interpretation.

To 'offer' a bribe may have sounded straightforward when you were first at the Infernal Infants School, but even your limited experience will have shown the spectrum of meanings that it hides. There was a time when this was not so. In days gone by, it was possible for us to approach humans openly and dressed in full regalia, holding out an inducement such as a suitable quality of bearer bonds, convertible stock or young females, in exchange for whatever evil was desired; preferably for the individual's soul. The All Lowest Himself found this an ideal form of relaxation; stories about his achievements are still told in the bars of ICM.

Sadly, these days have gone. If you were to appear in Buckden's office in your uniform of Probationary Tempter, and say 'Buckden, I have here one million ecus. In exchange, I will accept either your soul or the secret formula for the latest gnome plastic,' he would merely smile distantly, and ask his secretary to show you the way to the Staff Association rehearsal room. The only meaning he would attach to the word 'soul' is a kind of American pop music. We also now have to cope with that pestiferous body – OFFTEMPT (The Office of Fair Temptation).

OFFTEMPT was set up following a particularly tense meeting of the Council of ICM. An increasing number of complaints had been received from managers who had been persuaded to give up their occupational pension

entitlement. A group of badly-trained Tempters had offered a range of unsuitable inducements such as membership of Quangos, profiles in the *Financial Times*, life peerages, and even live appearances on *The Money Programme*. Whilst OFFTEMPT has no statutory powers, the fact that the CE is a retired Archtempter who still golfs with the All Lowest can cause problems; it is wisest to avoid unnecessary clashes. You should keep a written record of all bribes offered. I must also remind you that there is now a compulsory cooling-off period during which acceptance of a bribe may be revoked.

To 'offer' a bribe now, therefore, calls for a far greater range of skills. Timing is crucial. To persuade Buckden to part with the formula for the latest gnome plastic, you would need to approach him when he was least alert – at a jolly to launch a government initiative, for example, or the annual general meeting of his professional Institution. Except in dreams, appearance in your real character is out of the question; impersonation and disguise are essential. You should develop a range of suitable disguises; an old school-friend with whom he committed indecency; the current husband of his ex-wife; the Chairman of a company from which he was sacked. If all else fails, you can greet him heartily by name in such a way as to suggest that he should recognize you and that you know something to his disadvantage. When approaching CEs, this is easier than you think.

The nature of the bribe is all important. To be successful, a bribe must be:

(a) Flattering
(b) 'Tax Invisible'

Thus a fistful of used notes offered to Sir Andrew, whilst passing criterion (b), would certainly fail on criterion (a). A suitcase full would probably pass (a), but might run into problems with (b).

The safest bribes are thus the various forms of 'corporate entertainment'; the box at the Lord's test match or Wimbledon; the seats at the Twickenham international or Covent Garden. However, such forms of corruption, unless part of a strategic plan, are relatively trivial. To win the major battles, you must ensure your accountancy knowledge is complete, accurate and up-to-date. You have already attended the two-day Accounting for Non-financial Tempters course, but this is not enough. Without realizing it, the UK government has made our task harder; the annual accretions to its already labyrinthine tax regulations have now produced a situation so complex that even the best brains in the ICM Accountancy Directorate have serious problems.

Nevertheless, it is in this area that you must pursue Sir Andrew. You must grasp the fundamentals of the reverse cash bid, insider share dealing, reverse takeovers, the injection of equity capital and the creative use of pension funds. Sadly, my knowledge of such matters is now a trifle out of date, but I wish you luck.

It is sometimes naïvely asked why major corruption is not immediately exposed for what it is, and why those responsible are not drummed from office. Part of the answer lies in what you learnt from my fourth letter about the Sin of Clubbability. It is said, truthfully, that the All Lowest looks after His own; so do those the All Lowest has marked out as His own. But it is also true that those engaged in corruption rapidly learn how to cover their tracks. Together, these two factors produce the Whitewash Effect (WE). WE has been perfected to the highest levels by government departments and their agencies. It is important that you understand the steps by which it is achieved.

Let us suppose that a ministry has committed some grave crime; using taxpayers' money to bribe the prime minister of a third world country, for example. The WE will follow this sequence:

1. Denial that anything has happened
2. Claim that if anything has happened it cannot be discussed without endangering the security of the realm
3. Prosecution of innocent members of the public
4. Issue of gagging order to ensure conviction
5. Claim that gagging order was:
   - not intended to gag
   - was intended to help the defence
   - was issued by mistakes
   - was misunderstood by the judge
   - is not properly called a 'gagging order', but rather 'a notice intended to direct the judge's attention to matters more favourable to the prosecution'
6. Attacks on:
   - the tabloid press
   - the judiciary
   - the BBC
   - the Opposition
   - Counsel for the defendant
7. Claim that if there was any impropriety it was committed:
   - by the previous government
   - with the full authority of the Cabinet
   - as the result of a typing error
   - in the genuine belief that it was correct procedure
   - following full consultation with the Official Solicitor
   - on the instructions of the Royal Astrologer

Individuals within the public sector suspected of corruption and other forms of malpractice have, of course, a range of options. They can arrange:

1. – Suspension on full pay. This is the preferred

option within the National Health and Education Services. Unfortunately, suspension has occasionally been terminated; in a few cases after less than ten years.

2. Retirement on grounds of ill-health. This is usual within the Police service.
3. Early retirement or redundancy on enhanced terms. This is standard practice throughout local government.

In the private sector, WE is harder, and the steps fewer. They include:

1. Denial that anything has happened
2. Denial that the Board knew that anything had happened
3. Denial that anything improper has happened
4. Denial that the Board knew that what has happened was improper
5. Claim that what happened was the fault of a junior employee who has now been sacked
6. Claim that the Serious Fraud Office is incompetent and has in any case been penetrated by the Russian Mafia

The best ploy is, of course, to employ the right accountant. In this way, records can be kept in a form so complex that

the chances of discovery are minimal
if discovery happens, proof can only be obtained by years of detailed investigation
if proof is obtained, it is impossible for a jury to understand it.

There are numerous other aspects of managerial corruption, from fiddling expenses to industrial espionage.

Whilst you must ensure no opportunity is neglected, these are comparatively trivial. You should use Sir Andrew's growing paranoia about ICC to steer him towards the more spectacular forms of corruption. How nice if, before we have him here, he could spend a few years behind the bars of an earthly prison. I know now that I can safely leave this final stage in the hands of the nephew I have so lovingly trained.

Your Uncle

Barripper

Instrument 7: Corruption

INSTRUCTIONS

Select one option of those presented.

1. Slush funds are
   a) an evil to be stamped out
   b) a thing of the past
   c) a fact of life
   d) a necessary evil

2. Corporate social responsibility means
   a) a quote in the press
   b) delegation
   c) a full-blown policy
   d) paying lip-service

3. You last received a back-hander
   a) in the last month
   b) in the last six months
   c) in the last year
   d) never

4. Personal ethics means
   a) sleeping with a clear conscience
   b) not sleeping with your secretary

c) the primacy of bluff
d) not being found out

5. Expense accounts are
   a) to be used only when needed
   b) a perk of the job
   c) to be monitored vigilantly
   d) to be stretched to the limit

6. In payment scheduling, small businesses
   a) are like any other
   b) come first
   c) come last
   d) are an opportunity to turn the screw

7. Corporate entertaining means
   a) unnecessary expense
   b) an extra holiday
   c) diverting funds which could be used more profitably
   d) securing new business

8. Exposure in a fraud scam would be
   a) unthinkable but unlikely
   b) possible but shameful
   c) likely but unthinkable
   d) the result of inexpert attention to detail

9. I would never sink to bribery
   a) for fear of repercussions
   b) for fear of reprisals
   c) unless my neck is on the line
   d) more often than necessary

10. Getting the top/staying at the top requires
    a) sacrifice
    b) sacrificing colleagues
    c) sacrificing my family
    d) sacrificing myself

SCORING

1.	a 0	b 0	c 10	d 5
2.	a 10	b 10	c 0	d 10
3.	a 10	b 7	c 4	d 0
4.	a 5	b 10	c 0	d 8
5.	a 0	b 7	c 0	d 10
6.	a 6	b 0	c 10	d 10
7.	a 0	b 10	c 0	d 1
8.	a 2	b 5	c 10	d 7
9.	a 4	b 0	c 4	d 10
10.	a 10	b 10	c 0	d 10

ANALYSIS

80 and over: you are a role model in corruption, and will probably survive the extensive damage you are doing to your organization, your colleagues and your family.

40–80: probably lost in the declining ranks of middle

management, you choose either the means or the end, unfortunately not both at the same time. Have the courage of your convictions; you can make it.

Under 40: not worth a snip. Either too good to be true, a liar, or incredibly boring. Alternatively, you might succeed as an accountant.

In the End

Sir Andrew was due to be introduced into the House of Peers, as Baron Gnome of Wetmore in the County of Rutland. The College of Heralds fixed him up (at a substantial fee) with a coat of arms of two gnomes, fishing, gules, supporting a remuneration package, or. As his motto, he chose 'Gnomus ero; gnomonicus sum', an untranslatable attempt to link gnomes, sundials and collections of wise sayings. He devised it himself partly to suggest a classical education which he had not got, and partly to make a particularly obscure reference to Secret Society A (see the fourth letter) presumably intended to curry favour with its members.

Two of his cronies (the only two who were both already peers and also able to walk without Zimmer frames) were laid on to introduce him. He spent over £10,000 on his regalia. United's PR department did nothing for a month but seek speaking engagements for him and issue photographs (taken fifteen years previously) and press releases about his achievements and forthcoming ennoblement. A celebratory dinner was arranged at Claridges for thirty of his most active sycophants and the few members of his family with whom he was still on speaking terms. He had had a new suit, shirt and shoes made to measure. He had his hair cut.

The first sign of a problem had come over two years previously. (Needless to say, Relubbus was deeply involved in the happenings. However, he chose not to mention them to his Uncle, preferring to wait until his plot had finally succeeded.) A junior accounts clerk in a garden centre in Aspatria, with whom Relubbus happened to have established a friendship, dropped a bent paperclip with which he had been playing. In stooping to pick it up, he noticed a piece of crumpled paper under the desk. Having nothing else to do, he picked it up and read it. It proved to be a note to his boss, the company accountant, making what was clearly an assignation for the following night. The junior accounts clerk had received a sharp reprimand from his boss that morning for lateness, and decided to get his own back by showing the note to the manager of the centre.

The manager, whom Relubbus also had within his power, recognized the handwriting on the note as that of his wife. In his rage, he sacked the accountant on the spot. The junior accounts clerk was instructed to examine his papers and, in doing so, discovered a personal letter from the MD of International Crafts Consolidated offering the accountant a holiday for two in Tristan da Cuñha. The manager of the centre called in the police, who made investigations at the Head Office of ICC.

During the course of these investigations, documents were found that suggested a number of irregular dealings in ICC shares involving its CE, Smithers. The Serious Fraud Office was called in. After over twelve months of detailed enquiry, involving several thousand hours of work by a specially recruited team of high level investigators and auditors, it was established that a secret and fraudulent takeover of ICC by the United Group was being planned. Smithers was clearly a pawn of a member of United's top management.

From here, the investigations were extended to United, and Sir Andrew was interviewed on a number of occasions. Several highly suggestive circumstances came to light. His attitude to the steady growth of ICC indicated a deeply wounded pride, and it was clear that his financial position had been seriously damaged. Suspicion rapidly fell on him, and it was not long before evidence of his involvement in the takeover became clear. Working with Smithers and a group of close accomplices, on all of whom he and Smithers had dirt, he manipulated the share prices of both organizations. Substantial back-handers were paid. Smithers and Buckden engineered that the takeover would result in massive capital gains for both.

It was, of course, not possible to make this known until charges could be laid, and Buckden's peerage went through without hindrance. However, Relubbus had cultivated a contact with a hungry reporter of a well-known Sunday newspaper, and dropped a suitable hint to him.

In the meantime, the United Group cashflow had been getting steadily worse. Two weeks before Sir Andrew was due to be introduced into the House, they were unable to pay staff salaries. The management of the group had already been totally demoralized for several months by an extraordinary exercise aimed at obtaining BS5750 quality assurance, but which had in fact produced total administrative chaos. On the final Monday, the Group's bankers called in a Receiver. For four days, he struggled to keep the operation afloat, but by the Friday it had become clear that bankruptcy was the only option.

Relubbus' contact on the Sunday paper did him proud. Buckden's picture was the centre-piece of the paper's front page, surrounded by a full and highly-spirited description of the story of the Buckden-Smithers conspiracy and United's bankruptcy.

The upshot was total confusion. Buckden's noble sponsors rang immediately and told him they could no longer contemplate introducing him to the House. Buckden's wife walked out just before lunch, forcing her way through a crowd of reporters and cameramen. At five thirty the next morning, police knocked on Buckden's front door, and he was taken through the crowd to a waiting police car with his wife's second best pinafore over his head. He was charged at Bow Street police station. He had considerable difficulty in finding bail. In the meantime, Claridges and Buckden's tailor issued a summons for non-payment of their accounts.

The trial of Lord Gnome on a series of charges of financial irregularity made the headlines for the first week or two, but by the third month everyone, including judge, jury and counsel for prosecution and defence were thoroughly tired and confused. One member of the jury committed suicide, and it was touch and go whether there would have to be a retrial. After a further four and a half months a second juror was committed to a mental institution and a junior counsel for the prosecution retired to a nunnery. A month after that, the volume of documents in court became so great that the trial was moved to a closed ice-rink in Walthamstow. Soon afterwards, counsel for the defence pointed out that the judge had just had a birthday, and was now past the statutory retiring age.

At the retrial, the Crown presented no evidence, and Lord Gnome was formally discharged. It was suggested in some quarters that this outcome had been engineered because no one knew the procedure for stripping someone of a life peerage.

Within the year, Lord Gnome disappeared without trace. Despite extensive enquiries in Britain and abroad, no definite sightings have ever been reported, although there are those who are convinced that he is now living a second life as a Russian Mafioso. Should any information become available, readers will at once be informed.